First published in book form in 2005 by Treb Limited (Publishing), Orkney.
www.trebpublishing.com.

British Library Cataloguing-in-Publication Data.
A catalogue record for this book is available from the British Library.

ISBN : 0-9546260-1-X

Printed by The Orcadian, Hell's Half Acre, Kirkwall, Orkney

Dead Right

~ life on an Orkney island farm

words by
Julia Welstead

pictures by
Dominique Cameron

Treb Publishing

Contents

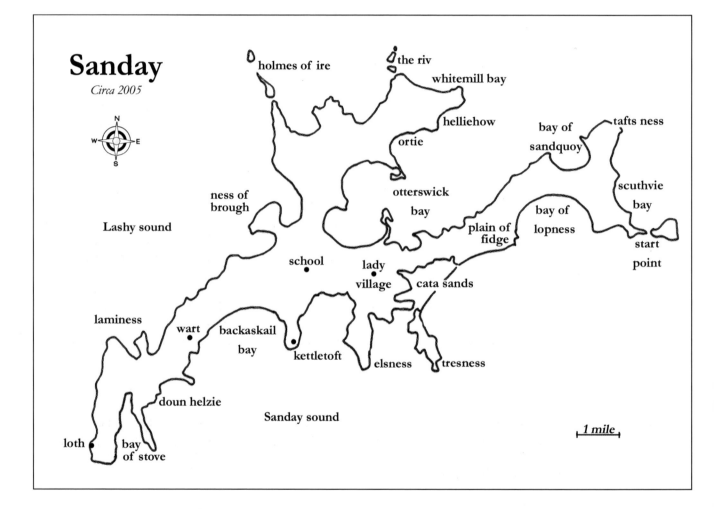

Sanday

Circa 2005

holmes of ire

the riv

whitemill bay

helliehow

bay of
sandquoy

tafts ness

ortie

scuthvie
bay

ness of
brough

otterswick
bay

Lashy sound

plain of
fidge

bay of
lopness

start

point

school

lady
village

cata sands

laminess

wart

backaskail

bay

kettletoft

elsness

tresness

doun helzie

Sanday sound

1 mile

loth

bay
of stove

Foreword

island: a mass of land surrounded by water; anything isolated, detached, or surrounded by something of a different nature

Island life. It's a funny old thing: sometimes so very different from mainland life and sometimes not so very different. The contrasts are easy to pick out - the sea and beaches that surround us, the space and beauty of an uncluttered, minimally populated environment, the clear, sharp tang of our salt air. The lack of a city, with all its attendant shops and facilities, to drive to. The time and effort it takes, via ferry or plane, to get to anywhere else. The wild, maritime climate. These are the big things, the easy differences to spot.

Yet even through all of life's routine mundanities - shopping for food, taking kids to school, visiting the bank - there is always some aspect or turn of events that reminds me of the remoteness of my location. It might be that a huge wave breaks across the pier to soak me through just as I approach the shop door. Or perhaps it's that my bank only visits the island once a fortnight and I find it so hard to remember which Tuesday they will be here that I no longer bother to go at all. Or the happy realisation that my sons are quite safe to walk the two mile, coastal road home from the school bus, with nothing more daunting than a brisk breeze and nothing more threatening than a rain cloud on the horizon. Or the delight of riding my horses along endless pristine beaches without seeing a soul.

Every week I write a column for the Saturday issue of Scotland's national newspaper *The Scotsman*. It is called "island life" and depicts just that, from my very personal viewpoint. This book is a collection of two years of those stories and observations of my idyllic island life with my four boys - three sons, one husband - and an ever increasing number of animals, gorgeously illustrated by my fellow islander, Dominique.

Acknowledgments are tricky beasts and I'll never be able to list all the folk who have influenced this book. Maggie the lambs, Marcus o' Faray, Sue the spade, Martyn the calves, Davo the plough, Kirby's Last Stand, Ian the farm-sitter, Sanday Fiddle Club, Irene the post, Tommy the fence, Mums and Dads, friends and family; you'll find them all, and many more, in my stories. Thanks to everyone who features.

For the material and production of this book, the following were essential:

The Scotsman for continuing to publish my words, week after week.
Dominique for her talent in capturing the essence of this island in her art.
Lauren and Miles for proof-reading my words.
Nic for all his time, patience and techy expertise on the book layout.
Drew for taking it through to printing.

Enjoy.

for my gorgeous boys - Nic, Miles, Dale and Fenning - for loving island life as much as I do

Red sky at night

~ Autumn

2003

Farming ~ *October*

Two winters ago I fell asleep over a pile of agricultural bumf. I was trying to find out more about keeping sheep, of which I seemed to have inherited quota for ten. Through the intervening seasons my ever helpful farming neighbour has helped me through lambings and dippings, tuppings and clippings. He has shifted my eleven sheep and their lambs from field to field when need be. He took my first four lambs to market last autumn. To be honest he has taken the sweat out of the business of keeping sheep for me.

Last weekend was my wake-up call - this best-of-neighbours broke his leg (not in a farming accident as you might imagine, but while playing inter-parish football). He is stookied from toe to hip and out of action until Christmas. So I'm finally going to have to learn how to look after my own sheep.

Meanwhile, back at the ranch, I have a stressed out businessman of a husband who is on the lookout for a career change. I may not be good at shepherding myself but I can put two and two together and come to the obvious conclusion. What Nic needs is a flock of sheep, twenty-four acres of pasture and two sheepdog puppies. He needs to exchange the rat race for a fine stretch of rat infested byres. He can while away his free afternoons re-building about 1000metres of tumbling dry stane dyke.

So Nic and I are now partners in the joys and worries, sweat and toil of farming. First we have to go right back to the drawing board, find out a bit more and make some decisions. Do we want to have sheep, or do something else with our wee patch of land? If sheep, should we build up a pure bred flock rather than keep the mixed bunch I have now? If so which breed? How many sheep will our twenty-four acres support? How do we buy and sell sheep and where from (the mysteries of the auction mart lie ahead of us)? Can we train our two collies to round up sheep - or will it be more a case of them teaching us how it's done?

I'm contemplating this when the urgent barking of the dogs heralds the arrival of a stranger. A man with a clipboard emerges from a town car and introduces himself as the DEFRA representative for our area. What? Another government department I have never heard of.

He needs to update the department's record of our holding. How many sheep, goats, pigs, cows? He explains the animal identification and tagging system, talks to me in acronyms - SAMU and CAPM and SEERAD. We fill out record forms and he promises more in the post - as if this will be something to look forward to. And his parting shot? "You'll be needing a passport for your horse by Christmas time."

There's more stress in this farming malarkey than meets the eye. Less hanging over the gate with straw between your teeth, more hunching over the kitchen table with a pen between your teeth. Thank goodness I now have a farming partner who can do all the paperwork.

DEFRA = Department of the Environment for Food and Rural Affairs
SAMU = Scottish Animal Movement Unit
CAPM = Common Agricultural Policy Management
SEERAD = Scottish Executive Environment & Rural Affairs Department

Sheep ~ *October*

Word gets around fast on this wee island. I've just had a phone call from a neighbour who has heard that we might be in the market for some sheep. He has two Jacob ewes for sale.

We already have three Jacob sheep in our small flock and they seem healthy and hardy and produce good lambs. The "real" sheep farmers around us are a tad scathing of Jacobs - they're not seen as a serious breed. But they might be just the thing for us novices. I put the decision on hold while I read up a bit more on sheep breeds.

We've come across a book ("Storey's Guide to Raising Sheep" by Simmons & Ekarius) that covers an amazing fifty-one breeds, from Barbados Blackbelly to Wiltshire Horn. I'm sure there are many more, but that's plenty choice for me.

I'm immediately distracted by such exotic names as Debouillet, Finnsheep, Hog-Island, Icelandic, Katahdin, Navajo-Churro, Romanov, St. Croix and Tunisian Barbary. But I must at least home in on breeds that are tried and tested to survive the Orkney climate and are therefore locally marketable. My serious list gets whittled down to Shetland, Texel, Cheviot and Jacob.

Moorit, mogit, sholmit, shaela, eesit - Shetland sheep are known for their wide range of fleece colours, all referred to in Shetland dialect. From white through fawns, reds and browns to black, this fine wool is used especially for traditional, hand spun Shetland knitted lace. By crossing Shetland with Cheviot (larger, meatier, excellent conformation) a good meat lamb can be produced. Shetland sheep are known for being hardy, thrifty and good mothers. Maybe we should go for a flock of these and borrow a Cheviot ram when needed.

Texel is a Scandinavian breed popular here for being well muscled and hardy. What puts me off is their poor flocking instinct - I have trouble enough rounding up our existing cross-bred Texel sheep. Jacob sheep on the other hand seem renowned for their good nature.

One website we look up has a photo of a young shepherd boy asleep against the flanks of a docile Jacob ram. Their list of attributes runs thus: prolific and easy lambers, good mothers, hardy and disease free, good feet, lean and tasty meat and fine, coloured wool. Even their horns are sought after by traditional crook and stick carvers.

We swither between Jacob and Shetland. Perhaps we should sit on the fence and have half of each. It certainly seems sensible to cut our teeth on a pure breed before entering the complexities of cross-bred flocks.

I phone the neighbour back to say yes please to his two Jacob ewes and suggest we collect them in the back of our Landy. Better to organise a trailer, says he, better for your Landy anyway.

Swans ~ *October*

Anyone driving the road below our house must do a double take as they spot a boy hurtling above the "tree" tops, vanishing and reappearing at two second intervals. This is eleven-year-old Miles endlessly bouncing on our super-kangaroo - the biggest outdoor trampoline we could fit in the garden.

We bought it in memory of our New Zealand trip (they have them in most campsites down there) and I can categorically say that it's the best "toy" ever. The boys are on it every day, rain or shine, perfecting their bounces, tucks and rolls. As well as helping with balance, coordination, confidence and fitness, it usefully bounces off some surplus energy (and there's always plenty of that).

Miles is especially hooked and spends most of his free time out on the trampoline. As well as bouncing he can be found lying on it like a hammock while he contemplates the scudding clouds. On dry days he'll do his homework on it, English essays inspired by the crashing of waves on rocks, or a passing skein of geese, or the wind whispering through the willow bush next to him. When he has friends round it becomes his den from which annoying younger brothers are banned.

Yesterday Miles was showing me his latest shoulder-drop double twist roll (I don't know what it's called but it looks amazing) when seventeen whooper swans flew over us. Having flown over they banked round to the west and came over us again, lower and slower. The circuit took time and effort - swans aren't built for rapid directional changes - and reminded me of an ocean liner trying to turn at sea. Were their efforts to take another look at the flying boy?

Around 20,000 Icelandic whooper swans migrate south to Britain and Ireland in October and some stop in Orkney to feed on the left-over grain in stubble fields. Most then fly on down to mainland Scotland but some will overwinter here, surviving on freshwater pondweed and winter grassland. Although personally I love to see them gracing our land and skies, I know that they're not entirely welcome guests. When the grain runs out they turn to grass fields, pulling up the grass by its roots and puddling the bare patches with their large feet.

Migration is a phenomenon that fascinates me and whooper swan migration makes for a fine example. Ranging from 8-11kg (with larger individuals on record) they are one of the largest migratory birds. The Icelandic population's 800km crossing from Iceland to Britain represents the longest sea crossing for any swan species.

They have been recorded flying at an altitude of 8200m (can you imagine the temperature and lack of oxygen up there?) and speeds of 140km/hr (swanning along on the jet stream). In fact, because of their high wing loading (body weight to wing area) they have to fly fast to avoid stalling. So those birds slowing down to have a look at Miles were risking a fall!

There's a WWT (Wildfowl and Wetlands Trust) swan migration satellite tracking project on the go this autumn. Swans who spend their summers in Russia have been fitted with funky little backpack satellite transmitters (with miniature solar panels to power them). These birds will be tracked on their autumn migration to their wintering grounds in Britain. Radio Four has made the brave decision to give this project live coverage - I will listen with intrigue to this, the ultimate in wildlife programmes - how does one follow migrating swans on the radio?

Renewables ~ *October*

This morning Nic and I fly through the clearest of autumnal skies in a Loganair Islander (eight seater) service plane. The perfect day for some aerial photos of Orkney's beautiful North Isles - but of course we have forgotten to bring the camera. We have a tight schedule once we land at Kirkwall Airport and photography isn't on the agenda.

First stop is a visit to the Orcadian print offices for a final proof check of my book (*Fine That ~ an Orkney island life*). After two hours of close attention to detail and focused concentration we raise our heads, declare the proof perfect and give the go ahead for printing and binding. It's a tense morning.

Next we whiz across Orkney Mainland to Stromness where there's a five day conference in progress. "Renewable Realities" is all about the harvesting of green (land based) and blue (offshore) renewable energy resources. Orkney is at the forefront of renewable energy research and development and therefore the logical place to hold such a conference.

Through the swing doors of Stromness Academy we can already see all the trappings of the conference. Huge posters predict oceans graced with offshore wind farms and massive red mechanical sea snakes designed to capture wave power. A map shows the electricity routes and renewable energy development sites throughout Orkney and Shetland. People mill around trestle tables laden with books and leaflets, nursing coffee cups and talking earnestly.

We haven't time to listen to any of the presentations before our plane home so we head straight through to the exhibition area (the gym hall of the school) and wend our way through a bewildering myriad of displays. Aquatera, Fairwind, Aurora, Ocean Power Delivery, Scotrenewables, Wavegen, Fathoms, Ocean Design - the company names reflect the energies of nature they are attempting to capture. It's all too much to take in at once so we grab the countless proffered leaflets and brochures to peruse at home tonight.

The drive and expertise needed to keep Orkney at the forefront of renewable energy development is plentiful. One of the sticking points highlighted by the conference is that to export power to the national grid Orkney needs increased capacity (new submarine cabling) across the Pentland Firth. But this information illuminates a counter issue - does Orkney want to become a massive energy generator exporting supplies to Scotland? Or should the focus be to encourage local communities (or even individual householders) to initiate and have control over their own power generation? And then there are the less "sexy" but equally vital issues of reducing energy consumption and reusing waste.

Our neighbouring island, Westray, is having a go at addressing the latter with innovative recycling of used cooking oils to produce bio-diesel and use of the methane bi-product of slurry digestion. Marrying these technologies with power from wind turbines, the 600 islanders have an ambitious and inspiring aim to be 100% self-sufficient, utilizing renewable energy, by 2010. Community controlled energy plans would seem to me to be a good way forward, with any excess power contributing to Orkney's burgeoning renewable power export industry.

I stop on my way out of the hall to contemplate a hydrogen propelled car. It looks a bit too sporty for me and I'm busy hoping that the designers will come up with the equivalent in truck shape when someone calls my name. I turn to see a face I haven't seen for twenty-five years. An old school mate, who, as it turns out, is running this conference. Small world.

~

Grounded ~ *November*

In an ironic turn of events (having written about them two weeks ago) I have had two close encounters with whooper swans this week. Setting off for a swimming session at our island pool a few days ago, the boys and I came across a young whooper swan. It was trying, hopelessly, to paddle in one of the potholes of our track.

I'll admit that our track does have such large and deep potholes as to be only negotiable in a 4x4 (and I'm beginning to think a small tractor would be handy). But they don't hold quite enough water for a swan to feel comfortable. We squeezed past it and left it there for the time being (as the lifeguard on duty that day, I couldn't afford to be late).

Once home again I phoned our local SSPCA (Scottish Society for the Protection of Cruelty to Animals) for advice. "Catch it if you can" said a resigned and weary voice that oozed how many "injured animal" phone calls he fields in a day, "and release it on to your local loch". He reckoned it had probably tumbled out of the sky after hitting the electricity wires behind our house. Having landed within the confines of our track it had no space to take off again, even if it hadn't damaged its wings.

Armed with the recommended swan catching kit (a shepherd's crook and a large jacket) we gingerly homed in on our victim. After a few failed attempts, during which it became clear that the swan was not injured but simply shocked, bewildered and exhausted, I managed to get the crook round his neck and keep his head gently lowered while Nic threw the jacket over his back and picked him up, wings tucked firmly in.

I then sat in the back of the Landy and nursed this huge baby while we trundled down to our nearest loch to launch him into the water. As he happily paddled away we thought "mission successful" until two, clearly territorial, mute swans hove into view. After some fairly severe bullying our baby managed to swim away, flex his wings and head over to hide among the ducks and eat some weed. I hope he's OK.

Today I actually witnessed a swan fly into wires and take a tumble. We were down on the beach when a family of whoopers flew overhead. Seven young, two adults. Then a twang of plucked wires echoed over the water like improvised jazz. One of the young birds crumpled and fell out of the sky, into the sea.

It bobbed to the surface and floated inertly, like a discarded hessian sack (young swans have grey-brown plumage). Moments later a head and neck appeared and the swan began to swim hell-for-leather, as if he might be able to catch up with his family, who had flown on regardless.

Home again and we are met by a bedraggled long-tailed duck on the track. I pick it up easily and we take it down to the sea for its blessed release. Our last encounter is with a snow bunting, flitting and hopping around the grass and gravel slopes half way up our track, which is obviously beginning to resemble the perfect shingle-shoreline habitat, rock-pools included. Perhaps it's time to re-grade it (I know it would make the postie very happy).

Aurora ~ *November*

Winter hours and our Orkney island world is turning monochrome. At the beach earlier I rested my eyes upon a silver-grey and diamond luminescence, mercurial sun glimmering through milk clouds, bone white seas darkening to slate in the shadow of approaching rain. I trod ivory shell sand washed by narwhal-white sea foam and focused on a horizon of the soft grey, layered silhouettes of far-off islands swaddled in mother-of-pearl mist.

Tonight Aurora, the Goddess of Dawn, has released her streamers of light and hurled them across our night skies to illuminate our world with pulses of light and colour. Or to put it more scientifically, the magnetic forces of the Poles and an energetic solar wind bombarding our atmospheric gases have contrived to light up the northern skies with an unworldly display of aurora borealis.

Aurorae (borealis in the Northern hemisphere and australis in the Southern hemisphere) are polar lights, caused by the astonishing voltage of electricity that can build up in certain conditions. The vital protagonists are electrified particles from the sun and gas atoms in our upper atmosphere. The former are protons and electrons which are constantly boiling off the sun's surface and into her atmosphere. Racing outward to her magnetic field they form the "solar wind" which pushes at our magnetosphere, compressing it on the sunward side of Earth and causing a long tail on the dark side.

Every so often a build up of solar wind pressure on the Earths' magnetosphere creates an electric voltage (of up to 10,000 volts) causing charged electrons to whiz toward the magnetic North and South Poles. The inevitable collisions with gas atoms cause energy to be released as light. Thus our skies are lit up with the flow of electricity toward the Poles.

Out in our yard this evening I whoop with excitement and yelp with amazement until the boys tear themselves away from "The Simpsons" to see what's up. We huddle for warmth and crane our necks at the phenomenal light show unfolding above us.

At the height of a platinum dome an astronomical firework silently explodes into a fountain of silver shards. Arcs of light and colour align and seem to mark out the route to Earth's Poles. Opalescent light sabres shoot across the sky as if to commence battle, then lose their edge and dissolve to darkness.

Aurora flicks a switch and a rig of stage lighting shafts vertically from behind a bank of cloud. She moves them like search lights to scan the sky. Then she plays with a gorgeous palette of colour, draws delicate chiffon curtains of ruby, sapphire, emerald and amber across heavenly rivers of silver and indigo. For a good hour we are awed, delighted and sometimes bewildered by the shifting scenes of darkness and light across our skies.

Aurora borealis, the Northern Lights. They are called the Merry Dancers here in Orkney and merrily, merrily have they danced tonight.

Tresness ~ *November*

Arguably the most spectacular coastal feature here on Sanday is Cata Sands. The inner sanctum is a wide, shallow sandy bay sheltered from the worst of weathers by a magnificent dune system to the east and the farmland of Overbister to the west. There's only the narrowest of gaps between this and the ocean at large and it is aptly named The Clogg. Water rushes through this ever-changing rock, shingle and sand clogged channel, in as the flow tide fills the basin of Cata Sands and out as the ebb tide empties it.

At most states of tide it is possible to drive (with a 4x4) out to the ness of land beyond Cata Sands. If the tide is out you can drive straight across the basin, if the tide is in you keep to the sides. So we are surprised, today, to find that there is no space for us to even creep round the extreme edge. With a combination of high tide and an onshore wind (wind over tide) the sea water has risen over the track and is bashing at the dune grasses and taking regular chunks out of the steep slopes of sand.

We could risk driving through the waves but short of a quick Lara Croft style conversion on our Landrover to incorporate a snorkel, this is probably unwise. We tried it once before and only got to axle depth before our dashboard lit up like a deranged Christmas tree. There's an abandoned car out in the bay, viewable at low tide, which bears testimony to previous foolhardy drivers.

Shanks's pony it is then. We're intent on reaching Wasso Broch, which will now be quite a long walk. For the more spectacular views we cross the dunes and draw breath at the fabulous oceanic beach of Newark Bay. The big surf roars and pounds the steep profile shoreline. Further along large boulders roll and rumble with the waves. We stick to the shore right along the east side of the ness until we trip over a chambered cairn (a c.3000BC communal tomb). It has not been officially excavated but coastal erosion has exposed enough to make clear what it is. I wonder what treasures, bones and skulls lie in the chambers beneath the turf and stones.

Out here at Chaldra Rock the sea is a boiling cauldron, wild and menacing. We stare out at the great blue yonder and stoke up with fudge before turning to follow the west coast round to the broch. This massive mound is also undisturbed by archaeological excavation. All to be seen is grass growing over scantily earthed stone slabs and wall remnants. A swathe of reed bed surrounds the mound.

Brochs are massive drystone fortifications dating back to 600BC and remaining in use until about 100AD. They were built like two-storey round houses with double outer walls, winding stone staircases, underground cellars and wooden interior divisions. At up to 13m high they resembled truncated lighthouses and served as the landmarks and prestigious houses for the Iron Age aristocracy. Brochs are peculiar to Scotland and Orkney has a wealth of them, including several spectacularly excavated and preserved ones. Again I wonder at the unexplored contents of Wasso Broch. But perhaps it's good to leave some of these archaeological treasures undisturbed.

As we run down the mound to head for home a woodcock rises out of the reeds. It's a bird I have only come across a few times here - I can't imagine this treeless island is its habitat of choice.

~

Auld Reekie ~ *November*

I'm lying in bed on a sharp November morning in one of the Scotsman's editor suites. I kid you not. But it's OK, this is no longer where the newspaper is created, now it's a luxury city hotel. Scotland's leading national newspaper offices moved, some two years ago, to a modern glass, concrete and chrome building overlooking the craggy beauty of Arthur's Seat and Salisbury Craig, down on the Holyrood Road.

From beyond our opened sash windows we can hear the muffled roar of a city going to work. The stop-start rumble of taxicabs, doubledeckers and cars on cobbled streets can almost sound like waves on a pebble beach if you keep your eyes shut.

As constant background musak we have the dulcet tones of Waverley station's tanoy lady confidently predicting departure and arrival times of the timeworn routes of the commuter trains. "The next train at platform 12....calling at Haymarket, Falkirk Grahamston, Linlithgow...terminating at Glasgow Queen Street"

Time to get up and enter the fray. Our window overlooks North Bridges, the glass roofs of Waverley, the East End of Princes Street and Calton Hill. There are people everywhere - striding along the pavements, shifting feet in bus queues, lining the train platforms as close as they dare to the "Mind the Gap" edge. More folk than live on our entire island are squished onto one of those platforms.

It's a gorgeous morning, cold and sunny. Perfect for a day of city walking. We descend through a warren of corridors and stairs to the aptly named Walnut Hall, which used to host launches and parties but is now the hotel reception lobby. Still avoiding the rickety lifts we chose the wide and magnificent marble staircase to descend to the breakfast room where a table laden with fresh fruit and croissants has replaced the cluttered desks of the Features editors.

Our walk takes us the length of Princes Street to Rutland Square, along George Street, down the steep hill to Stockbridge, all the way back up to the Royal Mile, down to Holyrood and finally back, footsore, to the Bridges. It's an irony of life that I probably undertake longer walks in the city than I ever do on our wee island. And I'm in my shirt sleeves all day - cities are so hot.

At night we walk again, down a bustling Leith Walk to the Shore for something fishy (Sea Bass and Halibut as it turns out). Next morning we retrieve Wizard (our trusty Landrover) and head out of town, over the bridge and North.

In Perth a rare kindly traffic warden points to our tax disc. Ye Gads, its two months out of date! Time to escape home to the sanity of Orkney. In Inverness we manage a little light shopping - a ladder, a cement mixer, a sledge hammer, a pick axe and a couple of shovels. Back home in Orkney a pile of concrete, sand, blocks and wood awaits us. We're about to start a new steep learning curve - building.

⁓

Collies ~ *November*

One man and his dog, one boy and his puppy. For his eighth birthday Dale was given a sheepdog puppy. Among his other presents were a book and a video all about training collies to work with sheep. We've all watched the video, been impressed by the skilled and obedient team of Border collies and taken notes on Lesson One. Now Tess is three months old and has learnt the basic commands of lie down and come back, without which everything else will be chaos. It's time to introduce her to our sheep.

Out in our front field we keep the dogs (Tess plus our two-year-old collie, Swan) close to us while we all contemplate our flock of ten sheep and they return our gaze. Here's hoping not too many neighbours are watching from behind their washing lines and tractors.

Lesson One involves allowing the pup to run toward the sheep and assessing her interest. For someone like me, who has been brought up with non-sheepdog breeds and the constant need to keep them away from sheep, this is anathema. But collies have to show an interest in sheep or they will not make good workers. The key needs are that they run round the flock, not through it and that they will stop, lie down and come back to you on command.

Our first problem is that Tess is so eager to please us that she doesn't want to leave our sides. Nic eventually persuades her to follow Swan, who knows the score and is delighted that we are at last letting her have a go at the one thing for which she is born and bred.

Next, Swan does such a good job that the sheep are bunched up and through the gate before Tess has a chance to get in on the act. She rushes back to us looking worried. Too many cooks seem to be spoiling the broth (too many shepherds spoiling the flock), so Swan and I retreat to the house and leave Nic, Dale and Tess to set off after the distant sheep.

I need something to keep me busy through this nail-biting wait until my book comes back, bound and glossy, from the printers. So I am once again wielding a paintbrush. Going, going, gone are the gaudy colours with which I emblazoned the house two years ago.

The eye-watering capsicum red hallway is now a mouth-watering butter yellow. The erstwhile emerald green bathroom is a beach palette of sand, sea and pebble. That soft grey-green colour of coastal dune grasses has replaced the bright blue of our kitchen. The floorboards of our staircase and upstairs corridor are a tidal race of clear blue ocean. I have, it seems, introduced my favourite habitats into our house decor.

My constant refrain of "don't touch the walls" and "don't walk on that bit" to any passing boys is becoming a standing joke. They dutifully tiptoe, hop and climb out of windows in their valiant efforts to avoid the current wet bits of the house.

The final pot of paint is blackboard black. This is for the hall door. No longer will my lists and messages be able to get lost under an unruly heap of boy mess.

Mud ~ *December*

Just before the Landrover squelches to a halt we get that sinking feeling. On our way home to meet the kids off the school bus we've taken a wee drive along a grass track I haven't previously investigated. But half way along its lower section it has suddenly disintegrated into marsh. I look at my watch - ten to three, twenty minutes to bus time.

Nic quickly shifts the transfer gear lever into low ratio and tries to keep moving. The wheels spin and we sink further into the mire. The traction control light flickers into life on the dashboard. This system detects which wheel has traction and sends all the engine power to that. Still we don't move any way but down.

Time to employ Diff Lock. I now know that this is a lockable differential joining the front and rear drive shafts. For normal driving it is unlocked to allow the two axles their independence. With it locked both drive shafts rotate at the same speed thus giving greater traction on tricky surfaces. But try as we might we can't get the lever across to the left. It's one of those moments when you wish you'd done that boring organised thing and read the manual.

On opening our doors it's easy to see why the Diff Lock can't engage. The mud is up to axle height. Still, we're not beat yet. Through the driving rain we can see a few old stabs (wooden fence posts) lying in the adjacent field. Keeping a healthy distance from the inquisitive bullocks we lug these back and put a couple behind each wheel.

I watch as Nic reverses on to them - yippee - and then both landrover and stabs sink afresh - damn. We try the old back and forth routine a few times more but it seems there is no bottom to this mud - was there ever any hard core on this track?

Three o'clock and almost sunset - time to make a couple of phone calls. First to the school. After my garbled explanation the secretary rushes off to stop the boys getting onto their bus home. She assures me that they can stay at school until 5pm - we'll surely be free of our sticky situation by then.

Next we must swallow our pride and phone the nearest farmer - could he please come and pull us out with his tractor? Nic walks back up the track to meet him and twenty minutes later I hear the chug of a little old tractor approaching through the gathering dusk. But despite his valiant efforts the wee tractor can't pull out our hefty landy. And with no lights, he'll need to get back up the road before total darkness engulfs us.

Headlights suddenly dazzle us from across the field. Another farmer and his wife (who happens to be our postie) have a good laugh at our predicament then head off to get their big new all powerful tractor. Even with this it takes a good few pulls and a broken tow rope before we get yanked out. A great story for tomorrow's post run.

Feeling daft, soaked through and muddy, it's 5.30pm before we limp up the road (the Landrover's steering is a bit wonky) and collect the boys from a neighbour who took them under her wing when the school closed. Next morning after hosing off a sea of mud Nic discovers the Landy's steering problem - a three foot stab through the heart of her undercarriage. But miraculously there's no damage - it missed all her vital organs.

Some hae maet

~ Winter
2003

Seals ~ *December*

Winter storms, rough seas and high winds are upon us up here in Orkney. Our yard is a quagmire, our porch a muddy dampness of boots and jackets. Nasty weather is an inconvenience for us humans, but for the Grey seals, who have just given birth to their pups, bad weather is bad news.

Seals (or selkies) are a constant presence in our shore and seascape. Wherever we walk, cycle or drive we are bound to see the bobbing heads of curious seals taking a look at us or the curvaceous, sleek bodies of hauled out seals basking in the sun. For most of the year we walk along their shore habitats and they keep pace with us a few yards out in the sea. But from late October through November we avoid the remote beaches, for this is the Grey seal pupping season.

We have both of Britain's indigenous seal species here, the Grey and the Common (or Harbour). Despite their similar appearance (but the Grey's have the Roman noses and the Common's have the dog noses) the two species lead quite different lifestyles.

The smaller Common seals were historically known in Orkney as tang-fish because they are seen in and around the inshore waters (in amongst the seaweed) all year round. They are, despite their name, less common than the Grey's with about 8,000 (5% of the world population) in Orkney. Because it would be nigh on impossible to count seals from the ground, populations are surveyed from the air using thermal imaging techniques (put simply, warm bodies show up on the image and can be counted).

Common seals produce their young in June in simple fashion. The mother will haul out onto a sandbank at high tide, give birth to a single pup and both mother and pup will be off to sea again on the next high tide. Common seal pups shed their white baby pelts while still in the womb and thus emerge already sea-worthy in their adult grey-brown coats.

Haaf-fish or Grey seals are larger (up to two metres long and 300kg in weight) and Orkney holds some 54,000, representing about 13% of the world population. Their traditional name stems from their more oceanic lifestyle (haaf means ocean in Old Norse). Every autumn both males and females congregate at traditional colony sites on uninhabited islands or remote beaches.

Pups (again, only one per mum) are born in their pure white infant pelts and are nurtured onshore for 3-4 weeks. By then they have put on plenty of blubber from the fat-rich seal milk and have moulted to their adult blue-grey coats. As soon as she considers her pup weaned, Mum heads off to sea (she's been losing some 3.8kg in weight per day and needs to eat) and the pup must fend for himself.

Problems arise for the Grey seal pups when heavy seas wash them offshore prematurely. Then they get separated from their Mums and drown or starve. So dead seal pups on Orkney's weather battered autumn shorelines are a distressing, but not unusual, find.

Boys ~ *December*

Bringing up kids is wicked fun. Especially when the eldest is approaching teenagedom. My lovely Miles's twelve year old birthday needs (note they are no longer classified as wishes) are for a black-painted bedroom adorned with an eclectic mix of gothic posters: the Grim Reaper, Avril Lavigne, Middle Earth and Xmen2. He constantly plugs his ears with modern rock and he wants to play the drums. Weekends find him experimenting with coloured hair gels - red, green and blue - on his newly razor-short hair. So far I have only allowed the temporary dyes, but I know he'll persuade me in the end.

He'll persuade me because I've been there and can just about remember it. I used to have such short hair that I couldn't pin my nurses' cap on properly - the kirby grips had nothing to grip. There were various colour phases but the favourite was vibrant red - I can still smell the regularly gunked on henna. My teenage bedroom was chocolate brown. I had far too nice an upbringing to dare to be a rock chick, but I'd air guitar, toss my head and shake my body to Suzie Quattro whenever I got the chance. So I know where he's at and I'm thoroughly enjoying it (and his black bedroom looks fantastic).

Meanwhile eight year old Dale is getting seriously studious. Last week he soldiered on through the flu' bug that saw the other boys flat out in bed for two days. On Thursday, ghastly white and bog-eyed, he had to admit defeat. After a mere half an hour in bed he got up and paced the house asking what he could do. He built a mechano truck, drew and wrote Christmas cards, practiced his times tables, told me all about his Viking project, baked a Yule log and kept minute by minute track of what his class would be doing at school.

I rang his teacher, at his request, to ask for the work he was missing. As soon as Miles brought it home he devoured it like a starving tiger. When he returned to school next morning he presented Teacher with the two days work she had sent (assuming he'd be off for more than one day) plus next week's homework completed. He was the most exhausting patient I've ever had to nurse.

Fenning is a different kettle of fish. Although a six year old Primary Two pupil, he hasn't entirely grasped the concept of school, learning and homework yet.

What we learned from the Parent-Teacher meeting a few weeks ago is that he *has* grasped the concept of delegation very well indeed. When set a task in class he apparently feigns inability, bewilderment or ignorance until one, if not several, of his classmates and/or the classroom assistant will offer to do it for him. These are all things - drawing, cutting out, spelling, reading - that he is perfectly capable of doing at home. We deduce that he is working on his leadership skills.

OK so the mess and noise of child-rearing can drive me up the wall - I already know that in my post-children life I'll live in a spacious, calm, minimally furnished, house painted in the cooler shades of white - but it's a constantly fascinating, rewarding and entertaining experience.

Ba' ~ *January*

I was going to write this from Kirkwall, on Orkney Mainland. We were due a trip to "town" to see in the New Year with friends. We planned to get haircuts, catch a movie, trawl Woolies for some toy bargains (that was the boys' idea) and visit the Ring of Brodgar. On New Year's Day we were going to follow the ancient and wild game called the "Ba" which is held in Kirkwall.

The Ba' is, to onlookers like myself, one of those crazy traditional street games with no obvious rules and plenty of scope for injury. The basic idea runs thus: two teams compete for possession of one ball which, thrown to the teams in the centre of town has to be transported to either the top or the bottom of town. In Kirkwall, where the game is played every Christmas Day and again every New Year's Day, the teams are the Doonies (or "Doon-the-Gates - those born north of the St. Magnus Cathedral gates) and the Uppies (those born south of the Cathedral gates). An essentially male sport (would women do anything so daft?) there's a boys' game and a men's game on each day.

The Ba' is a beautifully crafted leather ball, handstitched strips of alternating tan and black leather encasing cork dust (the cork gives the ball a good weight yet insures that it floats if the Doonies achieve their goal of getting it into the harbour waters). With a circumference of about 28 inches and a weight of about 3lbs, the ba' has the disconcerting weight and feel of a human head. This lends weight to the theory that the game did indeed originate with wild Norsemen kicking the head of an enemy around their streets. As the winner gets to keep his ba', four new ones are made each year by a few honoured Orcadian craftsmen.

So the ball is thrown up and a kind of rolling rugby maul ensues (there's no limit on the number of players) along the narrow streets and lanes, spectators following at their peril. Shop fronts are barricaded with thick wooden bars and there's an unusual absence of parked cars. Every so often someone crawls under legs and breaks free to run the length of a street before being tackled by a new bunch of boys.

Eventually a winner will emerge to run the ba' to his team's goal - the harbour for the Doonies or the top of town for the Uppies. Considering the nature of the game, there are surprisingly few injuries - one has to assume that there are unwritten rules passed on and honoured by successive generations. Having said that, one man ended up with 14 stitches for his head wound this Christmas.

Our trip was planned before we looked up the forecast on the Internet, which turned out to be a bit blowy over New Year. It doesn't do to make a fuss of a touch of bad weather up here - you'd never get anything done if you kept too close an eye on the forecast. But there are times when it is wise to pay heed to gale warnings. There are times when it's best just to be home, battening down the hatches and keeping an eye on the roofs, the outbuildings and the animals. There are times when you want to be tucked up in your own cosy bed of a stormy night.

And the Ba? Well Nic kindly looked it up on the Orcadian website and we printed off the extensive roll of photos to peruse from the warmth of our fireside. The Doonie boys won the New Year Ba', splashing into the harbour after a 31/4 hour battle. For the men the Uppies were the winners, touching their goal (Mackieson's Corner) some four hours after the ba' was thrown up. Definitely a sport you want to be on site for though - the atmosphere of competitive adrenaline and the thrill of the chase is hard to capture on camera.

Tafts Ness 1 ~ *January*

Tafts Ness. The north-eastern extreme of our wee, sandy, Orkney island. The tail of the dragon. I park at the farm of Tafts and prepare for a cold wet walk - cosy new ear-warmer and socks from Orkney Angora, wellies, waterproof trews and jacket - I may like being at one with the great outdoors, but only if I'm warm enough.

Swan and Tess - our collie dogs - and I set off along the rocky coastline of the ness, keeping seaward of the farm fence and any possible cow interactions. Cows and calves are being separated here just now and they're not a happy bunch.

We keep up a fast pace along the rough grass of the coastal track, a south-westerly wind speeding us from behind. Sooner than I imagined, we have covered a couple of kilometres and reached the northerly tip of this ness. I look back across a uniquely boggy yet sandy landscape, dotted with transient winter lochans and crowned by the now distant Tafts farm buildings. Standing clear and high on a rocky outcrop, the jumbled rust-red roofs of her outbuildings resemble not so much a crown as a crusty carbuncle on pock-marked skin. This is a barren, empty and lonely land.

I turn my eyes back to the sea. The offshore wind is pushing the heavy, incoming waves up and back until they rebel with an angry smash down onto the great, flat slabs of grey rock on the lower shore. The upper shore is heaped with sea-worn boulders and brown-dead wracks of tangled seaweed. Fulmars and great black-backed gulls wheel silently over our heads. At intervals along the vulnerable, sandy, coastal edge are dump sites of varying vintage.

Broken wooden pallets and plastic fish boxes, perished tractor tyres, a buckled sit-up-and-beg pushbike, a neatly rolled up-and-over metal garage door, ancient engine parts and the inevitable unpaired, lonesome shoe that always makes you wonder about its owner. The saddest thing I find is the navy-blue remnants of a carry-cot, its mangled undercarriage a few yards away. Although unsightly, it's obvious that the rusted coils of fence-wire knitted through with dune grasses are helping to keep the coast intact.

Further round, rock gives way to sand for a short stretch. Sanderlings and plovers flit round in orderly circuits between feeding bouts. I'm busy calling the dogs off a rancid seal carcass when Tess gives a yelp and vanishes back up the coast at high speed. Re-focussing I see that the dappled iron grey and silver boulders strewn across the beach have big round eyes. We've walked into a group of sleeping seals without anyone - neither them nor us - noticing.

Adults flip expertly into the water but the half-grown pups innocently stay put and stare at us. Damn. Having carefully avoided seal beaches during their pupping season (October through to December) I'm fed-up that we've disturbed one now. Swan and I scarper up to the dune-edge out of their sight, then go in search of Tess, who is cowering in a sandy dip some 500yards back. She's unhurt, but obviously got a big fright and stays heel-to-toe with me for the rest of the walk.

Ten minutes later, from the very point of the ness, we can look back along the shoreline to that wee scrap of a beach and see that the seals are all hauled out again and checking on their pups. Phew, no harm done.

Tafts Ness 2 ~ *January*

Standing on the desolate north-east point of Sanday, a stiff south-westerly wind pushing at my back, I lift my eyes to the view - an inspiring panorama of sea and distant islands.

To my left the two lighthouses of North Ronaldsay, one retired, one working, mark her flat landscape. Closer and to my right are the vertical stripes of our island's lighthouse, standing clear and tall on Start Point. From this coast it is possible to make out the distinctive red sandstone cliffs of Fair Isle, some 25 miles to our north-east and half way to Shetland. Scanning the horizon with binoculars I think I can see far off islands several times but realise they are merely big ocean waves momentarily posing as land. Ach well, it's maybe not a clear enough sky for a view of Fair Isle today.

The dogs and I head into the wind, down the east side of this remote and lonely Tafts Ness. Off the rocky coastline flotillas of eiders croon as they duck and dive through the choppy waters. Dull winter brown-black shags colonise the skerries. Turnstones, ringed plovers and oystercatchers forage along the rocks and seaweed of the shore.

Along this remote stretch of land lies one of the least disturbed and therefore best preserved complexes of cairns and enclosures in Orkney. The land here is an unusual combination of water-logged yet sandy, which has served to effectively look after a plethora of the remnants of a pre-historic era. An archaeological wonder land: because it has not been exhaustively excavated there remains doubt as to what, exactly, is here. Three large mounds (each roughly 30metres diameter and 3metres high) are probably burial cairns, but they may or may not be chambered and two of them are topped by upright slabs of stone suggestive of more recent domestic occupation.

More than 300 smaller cairns are probably burial sites (one is exposed to show a cist within). Then there's one long rectilinear mound in the centre of the area and several enclosure banks make patterns across the whole ness. Walking through the area on this wet and wind-driven day it's not as easy to make out these features as I imagined when I read up on it back home. The mounds aren't as defined as the Teletubby's hill-home and the enclosures don't form an obvious patchwork of territories. But after a while my search image zones in on parallel standing rock-slabs, the lumps and bumps of the mounds and some protruding sections of once-organised stonework. Still, I'd love an aerial view.

At the beautiful sands of the Bay of Sowerdie we turn inland. Sand balances like snow along the lengths of the thick wire-leaves of the marram grass. Obviously no-one has walked through here since the last storm blew slews of sand up to fill the air and land on the grass. As we reach the rusty barbed fence a pair of fierce, yellow eyes pierce us from a dune hollow. Tess leaps into my arms in alarm as an unusually large black and white cat unfolds and makes a swift exit. Swan gives half-hearted chase, turning with prompt relief when I call her back.

We return to the road via Galilee: not the religious settlement of ancient Palestine but its Orkney namesake - a sadly derelict hamlet of thick-walled stone cottages. Perhaps it was a fishing village. Along the mile of road between us and our landrover we race the incoming rain and unwittingly chase a large black cow. She's out of her field eating the rich pickings of the grass verge and there's no way she's going to let us past.

~

Suffolks ~ *January*

It's a chill-you-to-the-bone harsh January morning. As I walk across the yard to my neighbour's lambing sheds I zip my fleecy right up to my chin and yank my hat further down over my ears. I have asked if I can come and have a look at their newborn Suffolk lambs. Painted onto the gable-end of the old stone-built byre is a football goal - this family are fanatics. In fact the shepherdess who is about to show me her lambs is also the island's football coach. That's when she's not supply teaching at our Junior High school, or taking recorder classes, or teaching piano in her farmhouse kitchen, or doing the myriad other community and home tasks that she takes on. Island life, and small community life, turns you into a multi-tasker like nothing and nowhere else can.

I duck slightly to enter the top byre. These old Orcadian outbuildings always seem to have low doorways. Inside there's an initial relief from the biting wind, but it's not much warmer really. Maggie, clad in farmer's uniform - boiler suit, wellies, mud - greets me with a cheery, "aye, aye" while holding a scrawny black lamb up by its front legs. It bleats enquiringly as she puts it onto the weighing scales. 2.5kg - at four days old that's a peedie (small) lamb right enough. Most Suffolk lambs weigh in at between 3kg and 8kg at birth. But this orphan is keen on her bottled milk, so she should survive, thrive and grow, with Maggie's ministrations.

Although obviously not native to Orkney - they couldn't come from much further away within Britain - Suffolks are an increasingly popular sheep breed up here for their chunkier, meatier conformation. But they are not hardy, so to produce a good meat lamb many farmers will keep a flock of hardy-breed ewes and put them to a Suffolk ram. This farm has built up a flock of pure-bred Suffolks and successfully sells ram-lambs to mixed flock farmers. A real accolade is when another pure-breed farmer chooses to buy your ram-lamb - that's when you get into the big prices too.

The downside of keeping a non-hardy breed is that they take a lot of looking after. Put to the ram on 7th August (it's that precise) these girls are brought in to their lambing sheds in December, start lambing on New Year's Day (does this curtail the farmer's Hogmanay celebrations? probably not) and don't get back out to their pasture until warmth and a Spring bite on the grass allows it - nigh on Easter.

Meanwhile they need constant care. Every day their cosy stalls are mucked out and re-bedded with straw and their constant flow water bowls are checked. Their mainstay diet of silage is augmented by an array of supplements. Mums-in-waiting are given extra calcium, glucose, vitamins and minerals (products with such descriptive names as "Multilamb Rapid"). Lambs are given colostrum at birth - either from their ewe or from a bottle. Then there's a dose of Vitamin E for each and a shot of "Kick Start" (sugars, minerals and vitamins) for those that look as if they need it. Even those lambs who are sooking properly from their Mums also get a top up of bottled milk. At around two weeks old the lambs will be given access to a cereal and mineral feed (weirdly called "Creep").

The list goes on. There's antibiotics for any signs of pneumonia and "Orojet" for a nasty sounding disease called "rattle belly". It's an expensive business, but worth it for the great lambs that result. And the early start to lambing ensures that these lambs fetch the best prices at the June Mart (Auction Market) sales.

As we pass along the wooden walkways between pens, Maggie points out a large and handsome lamb. He has a broad forehead, floppy ears, wrinkly nose and deep wrinkles of black skin all down his body predicting plenty of room for growth. A fine fellow indeed, the makings of a champion perhaps.

Back in the house I am shown into the living room to watch some TV. It's a thrilling episode of "Lambing 2004": CCTV cameras set up in the byre enables these farmers to watch their flock from the comfort of their sofa.

RSS ~ *February*

Our kitchen table is awash with agricultural bumf again. The closing date to apply for RSS, the Rural Stewardship Scheme, is the end of March and we have decided to go for it for our wee twenty-two acre farm. When I submitted an application to the scheme two years ago I did my own environmental audit, chose my own prescriptions for each field, filled in the many and various forms myself. Although the helpful advisor at SEERAD (Scottish Executive Environment and Rural Affairs Department) assured me that it was all present and correct, my application for the grant was rejected. Sometimes it's not what you say but how you say it.

This time we have decided to get a professional on the job. The environmental consultants available in Orkney, as suggested to me by SEERAD, amount to three. No wonder they are all so busy. I left a variety of messages with all three and eventually got confirmation that one, the FWAG (Farming and Wildlife Advisory Group) representative, could come out to Sanday.

We are busy convincing Fenning that it really is Monday and he really does have to go to school when a Vauxhall Frontera bumps and splashes its way up our track. Hazel, our tall and smiling FWAG rep. is just what we need. Her presence silences Fenning's protests and Nic has him jacketed, school-bagged and off to the bus before he can find his voice again. We contemplate the farm map over coffee and chocolate brownies then don wellies and warm things and head out to inspect the fields.

Two hours later Hazel has come up with a clever plan of action, making best use of the wet bits, dry bits and awkward bits to create a mosaic of habitats enhanced for birds and wildflowers while also allowing for stock grazing and hay cutting.

The key tasks are fencing (shifting old ones and erecting new ones to cordon off delicate habitats and archaeological sites), ditching (to keep the wet bits wetter and the dry bits drier) and hedging (for shelter and good bird habitat). All good hard work for us. She heads off for the boat with a promise of a draft plan in the post by next week. Genius.

Thank goodness the site visit for our environmental audit was before the great snow storm. Yesterday, with the wind building up to gale force and the sky laden white with snow clouds, the boys were sent home from school immediately after lunch. By evening great swathes of snow and hail were whizzing horizontally past our windows.

This morning we wake to a white-out. All the house windows - even our upstairs ones - are plastered with several inches of frozen snow. In fact the force of the gale has left more snow on the vertical surfaces than the horizontals.

So no school today and, by the looks of the forecast, none tomorrow either. We have fun with snowball fights and snowman building but I have to admit that I'm not best pleased. With a heap of work to be finished and a plane to catch on Friday, unprecedented days off school are the last thing I need.

Skiing ~ *February*

I have just discovered that islands don't have to be surrounded by the conventional ocean one is taught about in school. We've taken a boat, three planes and a hire car to reach Nic's Dad's home, way up in the snowy mountains of Switzerland, and find that his version of "island life" is one surrounded by snow.

We arrive into a starry night sky and drink in the rarefied mountain air while negotiating the ice-slip path down to our chalet. Next morning a blaze of sunshine wakes us from the sleep of a long day's travel. We are in a snowbound chalet, surrounded by others, some the pale wood of a new build, but most the dark, weathered wood and the rickety stairs and balconies of the old and the ancient. Some are homes and many are cow and hay barns. This village holds a small farming community (of about five hundred folk - roughly the same as our Orkney island) and is undisturbed, for the most part, by tourists.

For a backdrop to these snowy mountain meadows we have such a vista of snow-clad peaks as are barely believable. "It's a pity you can't see the higher peaks from here" says Nic, who partially grew up in this area, "just wait 'til you get to the top of our local ski lift".

The boys and I have been booked in for five lessons at the village ski school, just to get us started. Day one: we get kitted out with boots and skis and led to a small field about 100m from our chalet. The smooth white slope looks daunting enough. Our teacher has us hopping on alternate skis and walking laboriously uphill before the great downhill moment, crouching and pushing our skis into desperate snow plough shapes. Nic plays "mum" standing by to pick us up when we crumple, adjust our ski boots and hold all our discarded hats and jackets as we get hotter in the midday sun. Why doesn't the snow melt in this heat?

Day two: Miles and I grasp the balancing act that is skiing and spend the whole day going up the little ski lift and traversing back down the field. Dale and Fenning continue to crumple and get hauled back onto their skis by Nic or the teacher. By evening my legs ache and I'm fit for nothing but a hot bath. The boys seem unaffected and head back out for a few hours of sledging. What a difference thirty years makes.

Day three: after another morning on the slopes, when the concept suddenly clicks with Dale and Fenning, we take a drive to Interlaken, marvel at the glacial blue lakes then choose another mountain route up to Beatenberg (is this where the cake comes from?). The Eiger, the Monch and the Jungfrau: in the evening sun these famous mountains glow red. In this whole white mountain range there is one black patch: the North Face of the Eiger is a rock face of verticals and over hangs that even the snow can't cling to.

Day four: Nic takes me up the big ski lift all the way to the top of his local mountain. The view is stupendous. We make slow progress down the blue and red runs with regular pauses to quell my racing pulse and breathe in the silent beauty of the evergreen forest, the snowclad mountains, the clear blue sky. This is so different from our wee flat Orkney island.

My leg muscles shake as we make our final descent. At the bottom it's skis off and hoiked onto my tired shoulder for the trudge down the road to the nursery slopes. I'm exhausted yet exhilarated beyond belief. We are almost at the hotel and an ice cold Rugenbrau beckons - but who's that bombing straight down the green run? Ye gads it's Fenning.

I watch for the inevitable crash landing into the safety fence but instead he executes a perfect curve around to the lift, grabs the wire and hauls himself up to the next red tow bar then hangs on for dear life all the way back to the top of the field. Next I see Miles hop off the lift and jump his skis straight over a "jump" and down the steepest descent route, Dale in hot pursuit. The boys have caught the downhill ski bug, their sledges are abandoned and by day five Mum's getting left behind.

Wrigleys ~ *February*

Home to the Northern wastelands. Our Swiss suntans seem to fade within the day of three bumpy flights, an arm and a leg dash round Kirkwall's Safeways (it's amazing how fast you can spend money if you've a boat to catch) and a rough ferry trip. On the final drive to our house we're all pretty silent as we contemplate the bleak, cold, soggy, flat landscape of Orkney in winter. This is not such a good day to list the reasons why we choose to live here.

Our spirits lift as we negotiate our riverine track. The boys run and jostle to be first in through the front door. I light the stove and watch the flames leap into life while the others heap the porch with our travel bags and our Kirkwall shopping. Now it's time to retrieve the dogs and the post from neighbours.

By the time I get back the house is warm and Nic has cooked up a feast of chicken, steak, salad and garlic bread. A bottle of red is breathing by the stove. "Skyran" by the Wrigley Sisters, our latest CD purchase, is filling the house with fiddle music. Home is, after all, where the heart is.

Twin sisters Jennifer and Hazel Wrigley are among Orkney's best known musicians and have achieved international fame over the last ten years of touring the world with their fiddle (Jennifer) and guitar (Hazel, who will also play piano if there is one to be found). Luckily for us they have decided to cut down on the travelling for a bit and base themselves back in Orkney. So out they came to Sanday a few weeks ago to hold an afternoon workshop with us fiddle clubbers before wowing a full community hall with their evening concert.

During the workshop we were taught to play tunes without written music - my musically dyslexic brain was delighted, all I had to do was rely on my memory (oops). Jennifer also demonstrated how to get the best resonance from your fiddle by really working the bow, lightly and strongly, across the strings.

If you ever get the chance to listen to the Wrigley Sisters' music you will probably find it hard to believe the sounds that she can get out of her fiddle, the oceanic songs of the orca being the most entrancing and haunting. But I can confirm her astonishing talent, I've watched her put bow to strings and resonate her fiddle to the point of shattering glass.

Now, with the boys back to school and Nic wading through a neck-deep in-tray, I put the CD on loud and turn my hand to unpacking, sorting, washing and tidying. The fast fiddle tunes are rousing and I get through the work without any housewifely boredom. And then a miracle - the rain stops and the sun appears. Before I know it I'm outside taking a soapy swipe at our sea-salt encrusted windows. With the kitchen window open the garden fills with music.

Out in the byre a large green plastic parcel awaits me. It contains a dozen red roses - a Valentine's Day presy from Nic. But these are not the cut flowers you will be imagining. What I unwrap are twelve thorny sticks protruding out of round green plastic pockets. When I open these I find a damp knot of roots. Ah, brilliant, a dozen Rosa rugosa (dog rose) plants presented to me as root stock. I spend a happy afternoon digging plots and planting out rose bushes all around our yard.

~

Warsetter ~ *February*

I have a startling confession to make. I would have admitted it sooner, but I have only just realised it myself. The awful truth is that, on this very small and very flat island, it has taken me nearly three years to scale the heady heights of its highest point. In my defence, I hadn't thought until quite recently that it actually had a recognisable highest point. But of course it does, even the flattest landscape must have some rock or pimple jutting above the rest.

In Sanday's case it's a wart, or rather "The Wart", a magnificent 65m (195 ft) hilltop, with steep contours dropping all the way down its east side to the sea. To make it easier to climb this "massive centrale" there is a road all the way up its west side. That, in my defence (I'm feeling very defensive today), is partly why I have never been up the hill. Because the road leads to a farm and I never feel comfortable exploring around other people's homesteads.

The road also leads up to the island's telephone and radio station masts. Two impressively large and high-tech towers are copiously decorated with giant metal dishes which act like beacons, relaying all our digital data and voice traffic to neighbouring hilltop hubs to our south and north. Up on top are the wobbly fishing rods of our mobile phone transmitters. We haven't got an Internet transmitter yet, but it's in the pipelines.

Yesterday evening I phoned the current farmer of the surrounding land, to ask permission to take a walk up there and today we find ourselves driving up that road and parking next to Warsetter Farm. The fine old farmhouse is uninhabited, its rooms empty and silent, its walled garden overgrown with nettles, bracken and rhubarb. But it is far from derelict, the roof and walls are in good condition and the window-panes intact.

The big farm courtyard of old stone-built, slate-roofed byres is also in excellent condition. The one we, like naughty school children, steal into has an immaculate threshing machine, a well-greased engine and a sweet smelling hay loft. The whole place has the aura of waiting - as if the occupants have just popped out and will be home soon. Sadly this is not the case. The house has lain empty since its owner died some five or six years ago.

Less than 100 yards up the hill from this lovely homestead is the high barb-wire fencing surrounding the main transmission mast. At the edge of the fencing stands a beautifully built old stone building. It's an odd, asymmetrical, tall-hat shape with rows of holes through the upper wall: a 19th century doo'cot (dovecot) in excellent condition.

I think how fitting that the new communication pylons are so close to the old messenger pigeon house. The name "Wart" derives from the Old Norse word "varthi" meaning watchtower or lookout point, a place from which to communicate with the wider world (or at least find out if they are about to attack you!). But I'm told later that the pigeons weren't used as a postal system but for filling pastry pies.

⌒

God speed the plough
~ Spring 2004

Ploughing - *March*

I caught myself wondering, just now, about the wisdom of ploughing an Orkney field in February. Last week the sun shone and the air warmed. The darling buds (or bulbs) of spring - rose out of the earth and bejewelled our garden with nodding snowdrops and tiny crocus heads and the green shafts of daffodils.

The sights and smells of the farming world around us met us at every turn. Tractors trundled along our narrow roads, some towing the shiny blades of the plough and some the smelly barrel of the muck spreader. Fields, for either reason, turned brown. Our house filled with the heady aromas of newly turned soil (earthy and uplifting and redolent of spring) and newly spread cow dung (acrid and pungent but equally redolent of spring).

We took the hint - spring had sprung, albeit probably a false spring - and set about our own traditional seasonal activities. I dug over the veggie plot for the last of the tatties, onions and parsnips. Nic dug the barbeque out of its hibernation, revved it up and set up a couple of chickens on the spit roaster. While I scrubbed up the veggies for roasting, Nic was busy chilling some wine. Um...how much effort does it take to chill wine?

I eventually twigged that he must be up to something else entirely and went outside to find him trampolining with the boys. As the spring sun lowered to the horizon - at all of five o'clock - we lit the candles and sat down to a veritable feast around our kitchen table. It wasn't actually warm enough to eat the barbecue outside, you understand.

What a difference a week makes. Today all the schools in Orkney and Shetland are closed - as they have been for three days. The cause? Severe and sub-zero north-westerly gales hurling ice and hail and snow at us. This morning, not quite awake enough to appreciate the severity of the storm, I let the hens out of their wee house only to watch, horrified, as the first one to poke her beak beyond the doorway was lifted off her feet and hurled at considerable speed into the dry stane dyke at the far end of the field. I rushed to retrieve her and return her to the henhouse. On examination she seemed ruffled but not broken, shaken but not stirred, so to speak, but I doubt if she'll give me an egg today. The other ten hens obviously have more nouse than I imagined - they stayed resolutely indoors.

My plan for today (had the boys been at school, had the weather been clement, had the moon been blue) was to visit a neighbour whose cows are calving. He tells me that they have started early in the year (normally they calve closer to Easter) because of last spring's good weather. With early warmth the grass grew quickly and abundantly, the cows could be put out to pasture earlier and came into season earlier. The bulls didn't hang around either.

So now here they are calving in the midst of a snow storm instead of among the Easter daffodils. All sorts of clichés spring to mind - marry in haste...reap what you sow...the early bird (gets blown away).

In a momentary calm in the storm I whisked the dogs off for a walk down our track. That's when I noticed that the ploughed field to the west of the track had moved somewhat. And our track had disappeared under a smooth, deep carpet of frozen brown earth, decorated with a snowy icing. Quite what's going to happen when it thaws I don't know (a chocolate river?) but it looks beautiful today.

Calving ~ *March*

I take the last track on the right before the beach. Up through the in-by fields, goats on the right, sheep on the left. On a trailer in the garden lies the huge, bone-white mass of a sperm whale skull. An unusual garden feature, to say the least, but I'm not surprised. Our school's biology teacher lives here and dragged this off the beach especially to show it to her pupils.

In the yard I'm greeted by three collies. One big old fella comes to my door and gruffs and wags his welcome. The younger two are tied to the byre wall, in traditional farm-dog style, but they leap and bark their greeting cheerfully enough too. Not ankle biters, then.

The barking alerts Martyn who appears, bottle of milk in hand, through an old wooden door in the nearest byre. I follow him back through the door. Immediately to my left stands a bull, nothing but a metal gate between us. He's a Limousin and a handsome, golden haired stud.

Through another, sliding, wooden door I enter the nursery. Calves trot unhindered around their mothers, who are tied in stalls. Martyn returns to the job in hand - feeding a week old calf who can't suck from his mother. He points out the problem - a tongue which doesn't curl the right way - then hands me the feed bottle and before I know it I'm feeding said calf, who seems to be learning fast.

Meanwhile Martyn sets about tube feeding a wee quiet calf lying on fresh straw in the corner. This one hasn't yet mustered the energy and instinct to suck. She might have white muscle disease (vitamin E deficiency) or she may just be a poor doer. It's hard to tell at this stage and without the professional eye of a vet. With no resident vet on the island farmers here have to judge these things for themselves. They also learn to undertake many tasks - difficult calvings, castration and de-horning to name but a few - for which most mainland farmers would call out a vet.

Other calves come and nudge and nuzzle around me. Have I got any milk for them? I scratch their heads and stroke the silky curls of black or deep golden hair across their flanks. They lick and nibble at the tops of my wellies. Inquisitive, cheeky and always hungry - just like my own children. I notice that they already have ears full of tags. Martyn explains - the coloured one in the right ear (blue for a steer, pink for a heifer) has a letter denoting the year (like a car registration) and a number corresponding to the mother.

That's the easy bit. The other two tags have a unique code relating to each cow's passport. Calves now have to be tagged, registered and issued with a passport within 27 days of birth. Through the busy days and sleepless nights of calving time this extra paperwork can be hard to fit in. Indeed, getting the tags into calves' ears can be a risky business - have you ever tried to catch a calf with its protective mother intervening? But tagged and passported they must be, otherwise a government edict will prevent you from ever selling, moving, breeding from or even eating that cow.

About two-thirds of the cows here have calved, one set of twins, the rest singles. Most of the herd is the black, gold or brown colour of the Limousin cross breed, with a smattering of the white and creamy colours of Simmental and Charolais. Limousin are favoured for their good conformation and, not least, because they have pointy heads which makes calving easier. Having been shown the scary calving machine used to aid the birthing process, I can appreciate the importance of this.

Despite Orkney's unpredictable spells of warm winter weather, these calves and their mums won't be out to pasture until the first of May: Orkney's equally unpredictable spring storms can be severe.

New farm ~ *March*

We laboured and lugged, sweated and cursed. We shifted the mountains of sand and shingles and most of the expensive wee bags of cement and we finally concreted the byre floor to give the games room a level playing field, as it were. For this feat of building Nic wins best actor award for his hours loading and unloading the cement mixer and his patience and steady eye in the levelling of the concrete. Eight-year-old Dale earns himself best supporting actor for his talented destruction of the dividing walls of the old cow stalls - he's a demon with a wrecking bar.

Six-year-old Fenning's role was comedy side-kick as he obstinately fought over and guarded heaps of sand for his castles. Miles played reluctant teenager, huffing and puffing to deliver occasional wheelbarrow loads of aggregate to Nic on request. I'm afraid I can only take credit for my expert timing in the walk on parts ("can I help...oh, you've just finished...well done chaps").

Meanwhile we have been faced with a bigger building project. Our house has three bedrooms so Dale and Fenning share. In temperament they are a tad different (the proverbial chalk and cheese), so there's a lot of arguing over the rights and contents of a very small space. On Dale's seventh birthday I rashly promised that he would have his own bedroom soon. By his eighth he decided to extract a deadline of his ninth.

We duly drew up plans for a house extension and convinced ourselves that, having mastered concreting, we could turn our hands to building a few walls and a roof - no problem. We'll start in the spring, we asserted, thus puting off the frankly overwhelming task for a few months. To increase the sense of reality of the project it went on our blackboard (the hall door) list of things to do - phone Mum, buy loo roll, mend Miles' trousers, build extension, worm cats, book ferry for Friday etc.

Today I have a distinct "saved by the bell" feeling. A bigger house, on the tail of this dragon shaped island, and one that I have long admired, has come up for sale. Hurrah! Now my list of things to do says "buy house" instead of "build extension" and I must admit that this is a much more exciting prospect. But it also has to have "sell house" and that makes me very sad: to think of leaving my beautiful old house with its mature garden, its workshop and stable and byres, its 22 acres of grassland and its long and winding track.

Speaking of which, we've invented a new game. It's called "whack-the-track" and involves all of our favourite implements - pick-axe, spades, rake and lots of boy-energy. It was borne of the prospect of potential house buyers attempting to negotiate our track in order to view the house.

To me it is a lovely track, not least because it sets us way back from the road with all the privacy and peace that that brings. But suddenly I saw it in all its bumpy, pot-holed and puddled (we called the biggest puddle the car wash, so you can imagine its dimensions) glory. Now we have cleared out the side drains and ditches and we're working our way down the track, pick-axing the central ridge and filling the cavernous holes. By the time we are finished it'll be as smooth as tarmac.

Last night, after a good whack-the-track session we all went swimming to ease our aching muscles and cool our sun and wind tanned faces. On the way home the full moon rested huge above our eastern horizon, turmeric orange in its reflection of the setting sun and streaked with irregular wisps of thin black cloud. A tiger moon. With windows down we breathed in the cold spring night air and basked in the moonlight.

~

Otters - *March*

Nic and the boys were parked at the front of the ferry queue when they saw an otter. I wasn't with them: it was a boys-own (boyzone) bowling trip to Kirkwall, giving me a chance to re-visit my much neglected potter's wheel. The view from the ferry queue could in no way be described as picturesque. Massive grey concrete blocks are stacked up to form the artificial shoreline and sea defence for the pier.

The boys first noticed the otter slipping under, over and around the mosaic of concrete - probably a good habitat full of rock-pools and tide-stranded crabs. With the Landrover as an effective "hide" the boys could watch the otter at close range. After a while she or he jumped onto the road and loped across to the concrete blocks on the other side, passing within a few yards of several parked vehicles.

A friend of mine studied otters on the Hebridean island of Mull for his PhD. One day he was down on the shore focussing his binoculars on the entrance to the otter holt when, on the edge of his vision, he became aware of an otter walking along the beach toward him. Closer and closer it came. He kept still as a statue, binoculars still up to his eyes even though he was no longer looking through them, and hardly dared breathe. The otter finally walked right over his welly boot, as if it were merely another beach rock, and carried on regardless.

Sighting otters takes time, patience and luck. Otters don't have very good out-of-water vision so if you stay still and quiet there is a chance they won't notice you. Therein lies the key to successful otter-watching. Otters aren't exactly shy or elusive, just quiet and unobtrusive and wily. We don't see them often because we have lost the art of being still and quiet for long enough.

Choose an ottery place, classically a rocky shoreline (but I have also seen them on pure sand beaches). Then sit quiet and still. Read a book, snooze, meditate, dwam, put the world to rights - in your own silent mind. You might, of course, have to do this several times a week for a year before you are blessed with an otter sighting. You might find it easier just to live here.

Orkney and the other Scottish islands have remained a stronghold for otters through turbulent times. Back in the 1950's otters were widespread throughout Britain but farm pesticides and habitat loss took a heavy toll on the species. Chlorinated hydrocarbon pesticides accumulated in otter prey - especially fish and eels - and rendered the otters infertile. Since the banning of these pollutants otters have begun to make a come-back, but they are still rare.

While otters like to live along the coastlines and saltmarshes where they can find plenty to eat - fish, eels, crabs, frogs and even ducks - freshwater is vital to them for washing. Unlike seals and other true sea mammals, otters do not have blubber to keep them warm. They rely on their thick pelt of fur. If this gets matted by salt water it loses its thermal qualities and the otter dies of hypothermia. A secluded shoreline with an outflow of freshwater made private by plentiful bankside vegetation - rushes, long grasses, shrubs - is therefore an otter's des'res'. Sounds like mine too.

While dropping off Fenning at the school bus I asked our bus driver if she remembered seeing otters on the farm where she grew up - for this is the place we are hoping to buy and its land drops down to a beach. She hesitated - its a few years since she lived there - then a grin of recollection crossed her face. "They used tae stael wir chickens!" Well, that's something to look forward to.

Dawn chorus ~ *April*

6am. I am woken by a splendid dawn chorus. A skylark, high above my window, pours forth his pure and uplifting song like a fine Cathedral boy treble. Down below a blackbird counterpoints from under the Hebe bush with his melodious tenor flute. Lapwings warm up in the fields all around us. Peewit, teeoo, teeick, teeohuppo: their voices rise and fall as they flip-flop on invisible fairground roller coasters through morning-blue sky.

Our three Rhode Island Red/Cuckoo Maran cockerels lend their baritone cacophony to the operatic melee from beyond the hen house door. Three cockerels in one henhouse is definitely a crowd - I must find new homes for two of them.

The morning commuter flight passes low, too low, over the house. I hear the deep swish and sweep of graceful wings as whooper swans power over us on their way to their daytime feeding grounds. I wish they wouldn't fly so close to the electricity wires- we've witnessed two fatalities this winter.

Five minutes later I'm lifted out of a dream by the more business like honk and call of a flight of greylag geese. Are they thinking of leaving yet, to head north to their Arctic breeding grounds? Or will these geese be joining the increasing numbers that now stay in Orkney to breed?

Gulls - herring gull, common gull, black-backed gulls - cackle and scream above the throb of a distant tractor. Someone is out ploughing early on this sun-windy morning.

Gulls and waders, geese and swans, skylarks and thrushes: these are the dawn choristers for this northern Orkney island. No woodland and precious few garden species sing for us of a morning. I lie in the blissful warmth of goose down, drifting in and out of the last vestiges of sleep with island bird song calling me into the day.

Then the urgent kek-kek-kek of a bird of prey (sparrowhawk?) has me wide awake in an instant. Even though I know I'm not on its prey list, the sound sends alarm bells through my nervous system. However both skylark and blackbird carry on singing, regardless of possible danger. Next I hear the unmistakable woody woodpecker koo-koo-koo-ki-koo sing-song laughter of the green woodpecker. And now I'm awake enough to know I'm being duped. The starlings on the byre roof are having a laugh with their mocking, falsetto mimicry skills.

Starlings (stiggies or strills to Orcadians) are such ubiquitous birds that we tend to ignore or even be annoyed by their presence. As a first time mother living in the Hebrides I used to swear furiously at one particular starling (my bete noire) who managed to fool me, on a daily basis, into thinking my baby had woken up. The starling had Miles' baby cries down to a fine art and I absolutely couldn't tell the difference. I would run out to the garden only to find baby still blissfully dormant in pram and starling hopping with cheeky exuberance up on the roof.

Starlings should in fact be applauded for their intelligence and skill. Related to the mynah bird, they have an incredible vocal range and individuals can learn and memorise a bizarre array of sounds. I have heard starlings impersonate lambs, dogs, vehicles, telephones and humans as well as other birds. Mozart kept a pet starling as a musical muse, allegedly taking phrases from its repertoire when composing his piano concertos. Perhaps my bete noire has followed me from the Hebrides to Orkney (starlings have been known to live twenty years and more) and I'm in for a summer of woodland bird song.

Roly ~ *April*

I'm looking after Roly, a neighbour's horse, while she is away for the Easter holidays. Tonight it's 9pm before I remember that I have to feed the old fella. I hurtle off down the track, post a letter in the box at the road end and pull over at her cottage. Switching off the ignition I realise two things: it's pitch dark and I've forgotten to bring my torch. I have the most brilliant (excuse the pun) little head torch, but it won't help me tonight, hanging on its hook by my front door.

Rural darkness is so much more complete than its urban equivalent. Being on a very flat island, I can see distant house lights twinkling around the horizon, repeatedly overridden by the rhythmic strobe flashes of our lighthouses to north and east: North Ronaldsay and Start Point respectively. But there's nothing illuminating enough to help me find my way round to the stable. I switch the Landrover ignition back on and re-park to aim the headlights at the field gate. That'll get me round the first corner anyway.

Right then. Climb the gate (an old door propped against the dry stane dyke) then follow the house wall round to the back. I can remember a washing line at neck height around here so I walk gingerly with one arm extended up and forward, but I don't encounter it. It has either been taken down or tightened up.

My well-aimed headlights are shining right through the front and back window of one of the cottage's rooms so I can make my way across the muddy back yard without a stumble. Then I grope for the back door but instead I find a hole. Strange, the door's been left open - on purpose or helped by the wind, I don't know. We live on such a crime free island that I don't even imagine any other scenarios. I trip over the horse's empty feed bucket on my way over the threshold.

I know where everything is in the back porch, except for the light switch. I sweep my hands around the walls but cannot find more than a socket above the chest freezer. A strange smell pervades the room and my wellies slip on a wet floor. Never mind, I can feel my way around the sacks and buckets of feed, the scoop sticking out of one.

I wonder if Roly managed to open this door himself, having tired of waiting for his tea, but he's such a well behaved old gentleman that I can't imagine he would try. I fill my bucket with a double handful of molasses chaff then dip a scoop into the bucket of wet gloop of soaking sugar beet resting on the floor. An inquisitive muzzle pushes at my back. Horse fed, I shut the door properly and tie it with binder twine to make sure.

Back out to the dazzle of headlights. It's much harder walking through the darkness with lights blazing in your eyes. The harsh northerly winds of the past week have suddenly dropped to a gentle whisper and the night air is a spring balm filled with birdsong. Oystercatchers whistle their way home through swoops of whooping lapwings, the territorial drumming of a snipe and the lone piping of a redshank. The dusk chorus on a still night is as beautiful and uplifting as the dawn chorus. I stand out in the dark field for a while before reluctantly breaking the spell with the roar of my landrover engine.

My hands and boots are unaccountably oily and the strange smell follows me home. Next day I return to the scene in daylight. A large tin of cooking oil is upside down on the floor, entirely relieved of its contents. Open door, horse, spilled oil. The plot thickens like a game of Cluedo.

Ferry ~ *April*

We live 26 miles from our nearest town, Kirkwall. If that was all road miles it would take us about 40 minutes to drive there and I guess we'd find ourselves travelling to Kirkwall several times every week on some errand or other. We would get used to shopping in a supermarket, we'd probably take up a sport or fitness regime at the sports centre and we would certainly catch our choice of the latest movies.

Luckily (I think) it's not all road miles: its about eight road miles and eighteen sea miles. We drive the first bit along our narrow, unmarked, virtually empty island roads, enjoying the fantastic views across fertile farmland to swathes of sand beaches and sparkling blue seas. Then we park up and hop on a ferry for a relaxing and scenic boat trip, slipping through the North Isles of Orkney. Eday, Stronsay, Linga Holm and Green Holm close to, Rousay, Egilsay and Wyre in the distance. As we sail between Gairsay and Shapinsay we can see Kirkwall up ahead and gather up our bags and children, ready to disembark.

On a good day, if it's a direct Sanday to Kirkwall ferry, this takes about an hour and 40 minutes. But we share our ferries with Eday and Stronsay, so often find ourselves calling in on their ports. The longest route for us is when the boat picks us up before going to Stronsay - if you can find a map of Orkney you'll see why. The full Sanday, Eday, Stronsay, Kirkwall route takes about three hours.

For some people this journey time, plus the obvious timetabling restrictions - you can't just set off whenever you want to - is a tedious drawback to island life. But to me it's bliss. I love the remoteness, the inaccessibility, of small islands. I don't want a supermarket just down the road - I hate their hugeness, their vast ranges of goods, the bustling, jostling stress of them, their endless two-for-one offers and their mind-numbing musak.

Luckily, again, it's possible to get pretty much anything through our local island stores or via mail order. I have seen our hauliers trundle up our track to deliver anything and everything, from a 5 litre tin of paint to a twelve foot trampoline, without demure. When we do need a trip to Kirkwall (every couple of months at most) the boys (that's children and husband) go - they like browsing the shops, playing at the new Power Bowl, perhaps catching a matinee film. Lunch is a treat of delicious beefburgers from "Kirby's Last Stand - outside catering specialists" in Kirkwall's lorry park where Mr. Kirby cooks the finest burgers, oozing caramelised onions, we've ever come across. All this leaves me blissfully alone in a quiet house for a whole, long, peaceful day.

That's what's happening today. I have just had a phone call from Nic to say that, an hour and a half after leaving Loth - our Sanday ferry port - the boat has been to Stronsay's pier in their main village of Whitehall and is now sailing back through the Spurness Sound within half a mile of Sanday's southern shores. But, he says, it's a beautiful day to be out in a boat. On their way to Stronsay they passed under the full arc of a vivid rainbow and now they are going back under it.

He's getting a great view of the construction site for the new wind turbines being erected on Spurness. And, as the ferry swings south into the Stronsay Firth, they are suddenly engulfed by a rolling, ivory-white mist which Nic says reminds him of going under Niagara Falls in a steamer called "The Maid of the Mist". It's amazing where one's imagination can lead one, given three hours of idle time on a ferry boat.

~

Night trip - *April*

At eight-thirty on a cold, dry spring evening we get home from a session in our wee island swimming pool. I hang the wet towels and trunks on the pulley and stoke the fire to dry them and warm the house through. Then I notice the flashing light of the phone - we have a message. I press play. The voice, of the outgoing tenant of the house that we have just bought, tells me that she has finished moving out and has left the key on the workbench in the byre opposite the front door.

Yippee. I walk back through to our kitchen where the boys are demolishing several bowls of cereal each (anything to fill up their cavernous bellies) before bed. With tired concentration they scoop and munch, eyes down, focused on food. But they snap to attention the moment I mention our new house. We're all in wellies and jackets within a minute, unanimous in our wish to go up there immediately.

The dogs stretch out of their baskets and wag their tails uncertainly at the notion of a trip out this late. But they catch our excitement and jump into the back of the landrover with alacrity - always ready for adventure. We don't meet a soul along the dark roads of our five mile drive between old home and new. Through Lady Village house lights glimmer, a cat stalks along a wall, a dog waits patiently by a closed door. All is quiet.

Then we're out, away from houses and along the narrow, winding coastal road beyond the village. With windows wound down we can smell the salt tang of the sea, breathe the cold air, hear ducks lift off the strip of coastal marshland at our approach. Along a bumpy track (am I destined to always live along a bumpy track?) our new house looms out of the darkness.

Boys and dogs spill out of the Landrover and run and leap and laugh and bark with the nervous excitement of arrival into the unknown. With head torch on - I've remembered it tonight - I lug open the nearest byre door and quickly lay hands on a key. Nic has to unlock the door - I'm so unused to door locks that I can't figure it out - before we can stumble in to the solid dark of the house. The flick of a switch tells us that the electricity is off. The boys hesitate, but then head off with my torch, through the rooms and up the stairs, their whoops of glee, "this is my room!" "this is my room!" echoing in the emptiness.

Nic finds the fuse box, but before he flicks on the main power switch we have a look out through the kitchen windows. Except for the distant glow of the village we can't see any house lights at all. We're out on our own here. How wonderful.

With the power on we investigate every nook and cranny of the house then run through the byres together. The boys try to claim bits for their dens: the hay loft, the lambing shed, the stables. But in the end they're spoilt for choice and have to abandon their attempts at territorialism for the night.

Our route leads us to the beach. We huddle at the top of the grassy coastal bank and listen to the gentle lap of waves on rock and shingle. Then, frozen to the bone and suddenly overwhelmed with exhaustion, we jog back up the track and drive the silent night roads to our warm old home. All three boys are asleep by the time we get there. It's midnight before we sink into bed - for us country bumpkins that's way late.

Painting ~ *May*

I'm on a diet of Nurofen and dark glasses. After a week of painting walls white I'm suffering from snow blindness. Gone are the deep purple, the bright turquoise, the neon yellow and the fruity orange wall colour choices of the previous occupants. It took four coats of top quality obliterating white emulsion and my left arm aches from long hours of exertion. But it's done and our new house is beautiful in its fresh and bright new mantle. Now if I can just find a dark corner to rest up for a bit I'm sure I'll feel better soon.

The boys were a great help with the initial tasks. We took them to the Kettletoft Stores, in our island's capital village, and kitted them out with a boiler suit each and a shared tool kit of hammer, screwdrivers, wallpaper steamer and scrapers, paintbrushes and rollers.

They loved ripping out carpets and underlay and were delighted to be allowed to steam and scrape at the living room wallpaper. They even sloshed on the first coat of white emulsion (adults haring around after them to mop up the copious drips and runs). Then they discovered the rope ladder up to the hay loft and the long drop jump back down onto last year's soft hay bales. We have barely seen them since.

Meanwhile, for Nic and me, the first week of moving house has been a series of highs and lows. The house is big, spacious, solid and friendly (in my nightmares it had become pokey-roomed, flimsy-walled, damp, drafty and haunted). I have spent three times more than I budgeted for on paint. The oil tanker arrived mid-week and now the gorgeous white kitchen Rayburn is sending warmth through both the house and the cockles of my heart. The drains are blocked and the guttering above the front door has mysteriously vanished. The acre of ground next to the house has been ploughed and fenced for me: now I can begin to create a garden.

The barns are heaving with mice and rats: a bonanza for our byre cats. The house is also alive with mice: every cupboard is rank with mouse droppings. Six year old Fenning turns out to be a keen mouse trapper. He was unperturbed and happily unsqueamish about the "little snapper" break-back trap until he discovered a "keep them alive" style of trap in one of the cupboards (no wonder the population is thriving). He then decided he'd like a pet mouse and now I keep finding him clutching Tupperware boxes bouncing with the unfortunate captives.

His catch success rate is high, but matched, so far, by the mouses' escape success rate. Last night he snuk the latest pet, Fluffy, into the Landrover where it has now escaped into the realms of the vehicle's upholstery and wiring systems. This morning the Landrover has a distinct mousey smell. With Fenning safely off to school we set a cheese-laden break-back trap on the back seat. Sorry Fluffy.

We are moving our belongings from old home to new in small doses, by the Landrover load. The first thing we moved was the barbeque and we've been living on the hearty (as in bad for your heart I should imagine) diet of bangers and burgers, steak and bacon and a crate of beer, ever since. Next went the TV and a box of videos - exhausted by their hay loft SAS circuit the boys lie on the kitchen floor (the only wet-paint-free room) and giggle over endless repeats of Fawlty Towers and Mr Bean until we drive home to bed.

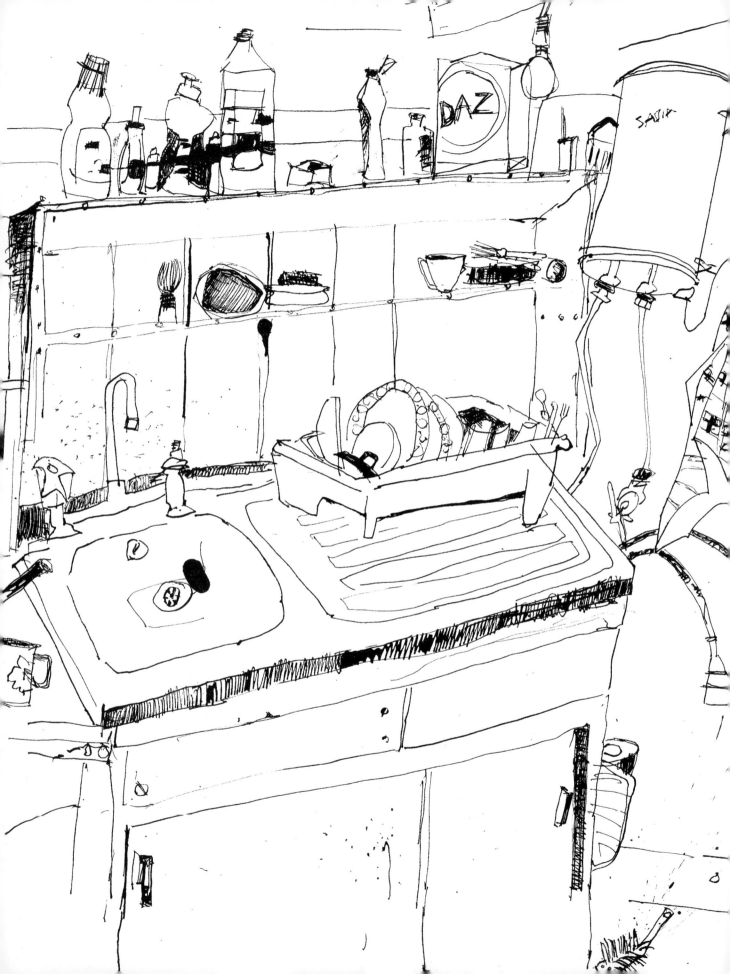

Music - *May*

"Ceilidh: in Scotland and Ireland, an informal evening of song, story and dancing". I looked this up in my dictionary today to find out if it said anything about the speed of ceilidh music, but there was no mention of music to be found at all.

Our ever busy Sanday Fiddle Club is holding a concert of ceilidh music in the island community hall tonight, to raise funds for the purchase of a Clavinova for the school. To break up my heavy schedule of house painting I swapped brush and roller for fiddle and bow to practice the reels, waltzes and marches on the programme. My music teacher and I went through each piece reassuringly slowly so that I could learn the phrases and rhythms and teach my fingers to find the right notes.

Then, at the club rehearsals, we were suddenly playing these tunes at an alarmingly fast pace with no time for hesitation. At the final rehearsal, on the morning of the concert, what with the general exhaustion of being in the middle of moving house and the muscle stiffness all down my left arm and hand, I think I can claim not to have hit a single correct note in time with my orchestral mates. That's when Nic persuaded me to spend the afternoon in a hot, deep bath with nothing to do but soak the paint off my face and hands and nothing to hold but a glass of wine.

Emerging from this steamy haze relaxed and rejuvenated I sort the music for the programme with Miles (who is also playing, but twelve year old brains and fingers definitely move faster than forty-one year olds, and don't seem to have the added impediment of fear). Then we dress in our uniform white and black fiddle club outfits and all pile into the Landrover for a rare evening out, renewed energies mingling happily with a handy pre-concert rush of adrenaline.

The concert opens gently with Loch Lomond and Highland Lad then we pick up the pace with the strident Caledonian March and Fiddle Club March. The audience sways (or I do anyway) to the lilting beauty of Bethan's Waltz, a piece composed by our conductor for his daughter. Then we are in to a set of Orkney tunes with wonderfully descriptive names: Maggie Watson's Farewell to Blackhammer, Partans (crabs) in his Creel and Harvest Blinks. I suppose technically these cannot be described as ceilidh tunes, the word being Gaelic and Orkney not being a Gaelic speaking country, but it's all rattling good fiddle music and nobody seems to differentiate.

Orkney has a long and strong tradition of fiddle music and the thriving Orkney Strathspey and Reel Society keeps the tunes alive and kicking. But, without such famous ambassadors as Shetland's Aly Bain and Tom Anderson, Orkney music has not been put on the international map. Things they are a changing now, however, with the likes of The Wrigley Sisters, Hugh Inkster and Pat Shearer, Sara McFadyen and Kris Drever broadcasting Orkney music, both old and newly composed, far and wide with their CD recordings and concert tours. I heard on Radio Orkney this morning that the School of Scottish Studies in Edinburgh has compiled a CD of music and stories called Orkney: Land, Sea and Community, an invaluable archive of the islands' music, songs, lifestyles, myths and even jokes.

Back at the concert and the smoke is rising off our fiddles now as we race through De'il amang the Tailors. In my brief research of fiddle music I have found no mention of the tradition to play the tunes so fast: I can only assume that the copious imbibitions of hooch led to the bow and fingers going faster and faster until they were fleein' along.

Flittin' ~ *May*

On the radio the other day I heard the DJ claim that his last house move took an awesome three days to complete. This momentarily confused me: did he expect it to be achieved in an easy afternoon, between lunch and the early evening news? But then I thought it through: in the land of professional removals teams, fast roads, easy access and no livestock implications, it probably is possible to move house in a day.

Not so here. Not counting the two weeks of driving across to our new house to paint it, we have now spent a good two weeks moving in. Because the two houses are only about five miles apart we decided (possibly mistakenly) to neither hire a lorry that would carry all our goods and chattels at once, nor accept several offers of tractor and trailer help, but rather to to and fro with the landrover by turn full then empty, full then empty, endlessly bumping along potholed tracks to the point of exhaustion.

First, so that we could still live comfortably at our old home, we moved all the things we never use (why we keep them at all being one of those inexplicable human conditions). We also brought Omelette, our favourite byre cat, because she is heavily pregnant and I wanted her to have the new kittens at the new house. We put her in the big, mouse filled, end byre and settled her in with butter on her paws (an old wifes' tale that has always worked for me before) and plenty of fresh meat and cream. For ten days she seemed content with her new home. Then she disappeared, presumably to have her litter in the peace of the straw bales. Three days later I met her back at our old house. She must have walked the five miles back "home" - whether by road or coastline we'll never know - in an amazing feat of feline ingenuity.

Meanwhile, between loads of garden tools, wheelbarrows, train sets, dog baskets, saddlery, animal feed bins, dismantled bed frames, crockery, bicycles, wardrobes, dripping plant pots and endless boxes of books, we managed to catch the hens and shift them to their new home. This, far from being a controlled and calm event, involved much flapping and squawking on the part of the hens and much sweating and swearing by us.

We caught three each, including the Colonel, our old cockerel, by grabbing them as they emerged from the hen house one morning. The others were too fast so the next morning Nic braved the interior of the hen house while I held the door and listened with amusement to the scuffles and squawks, the rugby tackles foiled by flight, the gentle cajoling and the fearsome threats. To be honest it was so hilarious that by the time Nic emerged with deranged hair and a hen under each arm I could barely hold the cage door open between paroxysms of laughter. He used to be a pin-striped businessman, but he's all right now.

For all that effort, there still remain the two young and strutting cockerels, who were just too fast and furious for us. As we don't need them (one cockerel per farmyard is quite enough) they remain at our old house until we either net them for the pot or offer them as a (not necessarily welcome) house warming present to the new occupants.

Two days ago we brought Omelette back, with our three other byre cats - Fred, George and Whiskers - and this morning she is missing again. I guess I'll meet her back in her old byre in a few days and perhaps I'll have to accept her determination to live there instead of moving with us. Cats, especially half wild byre cats, are truly independent and feisty characters.

~

Bees ~ *May*

A few evenings ago I gingerly stepped over a large bumble bee so that I could reach for a glass with which to transport it out of the kitchen. It was one of several we have found in our new house and our surrounding fields are buzzing busily with them. Our garden is still a ploughed field so not of much interest to a foraging bee. But the fields are full of flowering plants: clover and dandelions in the dry, iris and marsh marigold in the wet.

The next morning, in her 7.30 to 8am slot within Radio Scotland, Radio Orkney broadcast a feature on bumble bees, so I just had to stay in bed to listen to it. I learnt that Orkney sports seven or eight of Western Europe's 25 bumble bee (Bombus) species, of which five are common and the others rare. Probably our most notable rare bee is the Great Yellow (Bombus distinguendus) a species now only found in northern Scotland, Orkney and the Hebrides.

Interestingly this bee's habitat needs overlap with those of the Corncrake - a bird for whom habitats are now being preserved, created and managed in Scotland. Areas of long, flowering vegetation are needed by both species - for the birds as a secure place to hide nests and for the bees to provide pollen to feed their young. Bumble bees also choose rough vegetation like grassy tussocks in which to nest and the queens (the only ones to survive the winter as worker females and males die in the autumn) hibernate in dry banks, ditches or at the base of a clump of grass.

Bee populations are, distressingly, in massive decline across most of Britain. Orkney and the Hebrides remain strongholds for bees, possibly because we still have these areas of rough grass and traditional hay meadow fields sporting flowering plants (vetches, thistles, nettles, clover) that have been herbicided to extinction in the more intensively farmed central regions. And of course it's a mutually beneficial situation - as the bees feed from the wildflowers they provide a vital pollination service, helping the flower species to proliferate.

For all the bees I have seen in Sanday, I've never come across a wasp and rumour has it that there aren't any here. Personally - with memories of various wasp stings through my life - I'm happy not to see them. But why they don't thrive up here mystifies me. They have been found in both Orkney and Shetland Mainland (probably via crates of fruit) but don't seem to establish thriving colonies.

This morning Fenning and I whizzed up to our old home before school to fill the washing machine, which we still haven't moved (a long story to do with plumbing), check Chuck (the horse, not to be moved until he's shod) and feed the two flighty cockerels. Who should we meet but Omelette, our byre cat, looking sleek and slender. She proudly showed off three newborn kittens nestled on the straw bales.

On dropping Fenning at school I was invited in to see the "growing animals" display in his classroom. I confess I had assumed he was exaggerating when he told us of the variety of eggs about to burst into life in Room Two. But with some fifteen yellow, stripey and black chicks under a heat lamp in a big box in one corner, a large play pool of pondweed and wriggling tadpoles in another and a net cage full of foliage, caterpillars and cocoons on the side desk, the place is absolutely burgeoning with life.

I asked the teachers about the lack of wasps on the island. Neither could say there weren't any, but neither had ever seen one here. Then I was shown a wee box out of the classroom cupboard. In it was a wasp byke (nest) - an exquisite creation resembling a miniature honeycomb encased in a smooth oval wall of paper mache (wasps make their nests by dissolving wood shavings to make paper). The teacher's son in Kirkwall had found it and given it to her to show the children out on this wasp-free north isle.

Make hay
~ Summer
2004

Rotivating - *May*

The collies bark their "intruder" alert from their new kennel across the yard. I look out of my new kitchen window to see a tractor appearing over the rise in our front track, silhouetted by a warm, red evening sun. As it approaches the yard I can see Davo, one of our near neighbours now that we have moved further east on this wee Orkney island, at the wheel. A wide, many-knifed farm implement is attached to the back of the tractor. Fantastic. He's come to rotivate the ploughed field that we're planning to transform into a garden.

Nic runs out to open the five-bar gate for him and without further ado Davo manoeuvres the machine onto the first ridges of soil, lowers it to ground level and moves slowly forward. The knives twist and turn, shift and slice. A row of prongs behind them rake the ground smooth. Hordes of gulls fly in from every direction to savour the easy pickings of earthworms exposed by the freshly turned soil. Common gulls, black-headed gulls and herring gulls share the bounty with bad grace, screaming and fighting, bigger birds bullying their inferiors into dropping the tasty morsels. At every turn of the tractor they wheel up into the sky in unison to escape the fickle wheels and to seek the next feast.

Davo drives his tractor carefully round the perimeter of the ploughed ground then rotivates in long, straight lines up and down until all the plough is cut and smoothed. Every so often a rock is thrown up by the knives and carried along by the mechanical rake. I'm worried that these will damage the machine but Davo is watching over his shoulder and he drives steadily to the field edge then levers the machine up to let the rocks fall out. That's saved me a helluva job.

Dale and I run up to his bedroom - his south-east facing window has the best view over our putative garden. We're mesmerised by the transformation of a rough plough to such smoothly tilled earth. Dale is fascinated by the machinery itself and issues forth the usual steady stream of many and various eight-year-old questions that I cannot begin to answer. I'm dwelling on the hundreds of hours of digging and raking, the sweating and the back-ache from which this machine is saving me.

The final line of plough is chopped and combed. Davo turns his tractor to the gate and I run downstairs thinking he's finished. But then he sets off again, driving across the garden, and gives the rich brown tilth a final rake. It's such a beautiful finish I hardly want to walk on it.

The tractor finally leaves the field and I head out to say thanks and agree the price. Paying for work like this is hard with Orcadians. They like to do the job first then ask you what you think it's worth. In this case I'd say it's a priceless hour's work. Invaluable: or rather of incalculable value. I tell him it has saved me hundreds of hours of manual labour. He says, "Aye, but I think yer work's just beginin'".

We agree a price, me trying to give more, him keeping the price firmly at what he sees as fair. Then to top it off he offers me a couple of sacks of seed tatties to plant in the lower third of the field, which I've allocated as a veggie plot. Tatties are a good first crop on uncultivated ground as their roots and tubers break up and aerate the soil. I'll pick them up tomorrow and get them straight in. My work has, indeed, begun.

As the tractor rumbles away home along the track the red sun has dipped to the horizon where it appears to float on the meniscus of calm, blue ocean for a moment before sinking, rays of crimson cast across the water like ribbons of blood.

Cost ~ *June*

Our wee northern Orkney island is in the running for UK-wide fame - could we be the first place in the country to top £1 per litre of diesel? The price at our local pump was 97p/litre when we filled up a few days ago and that was before the news of further oil price rises. Our village shopkeeper and pump owner reckons somewhere else already charges over a pound. But where else - except perhaps another island off an island off the UK mainland - could possibly be more expensive? Answers on a postcard please.

For all my waxing lyrical about the fabulous quality of life here on a remote and sparsely populated island, I have never expounded upon the counter balance - the cost of living. I don't write about it because I don't really want to think about it. I have always upheld quality, rather than cost, of life, as my priority. But a rise in oil prices can significantly affect the price of every commodity available on an island, because it all has to be transported from far off lands across the high seas. Romantic, you might think, but costly too. We can reckon on everything costing an average 10% more than the equivalent on Orkney Mainland, which is, in turn, some 10% more expensive than mainland Scotland.

It's not just the price of fuel that we notice, but everything right down to the price of butter (well over £1 per half pound if you want to buy Orkney's finest) and fish (ridiculously hard to come by at all, given our location). Transport costs affect services as well as groceries. There's a lone schoolboy living on the beautiful, tiny island of Egilsay for whom transport to the nearest school - on neighbouring Rousay - is hitting the local headlines.

For the education authority to provide him with transport in the form of a private boat would cost £500 per week, even if they could find someone willing to run it. The alternative is to divert the scheduled ferry service that presently whisks folk efficiently between Rousay and Orkney Mainland. The diversion would put 40 minutes on to a 30 minute crossing, an option that the Rousay residents are, quite reasonably, refusing. I'd say there's a nice wee job there for anyone with a boat. Applications on a postcard please.

Orkney's rubbish was in the news today as well. It presently costs a cool £2 million per annum to deal with refuse from all of our Orkney Island households. A new environmental grant is being allocated to us to set up more recycling points for glass, paper, fabric etc and there's also a plan to give us all compost bins for our domestic food waste. Personally I hate those green plastic bins that you are supposed to throw all your veggie peelings into. The rotting process seems to involve very putrid smells and an explosion in the bluebottle population. Perhaps every household should be given a few hens - that's how we recycle our food waste.

To the end user, electricity, provided via the national grid, costs islanders the same as mainlanders. But the cost to the provider can be much higher. As an example, we suffered a "live hoose" last week, which we noted through the nasty wee shocks our bathroom taps were giving us. On alerting the local Hydro-electric man to our plight, he suggested we look out of the window at the transformer box atop our nearest electricity pole. Sure enough, there was the culprit - a crows' nest. It took three men (one boated out from Kirkwall when things went slightly awry) and many hours to get the north end of the island powered up again.

The nest was made principally of bits of barbed wire - hence the effective shorting out of the system. I guess crows are a bit stuck for twigs on this treeless island, but barbed wire? Ouch.

Manna from heaven. Great big beautiful droplets of rain are falling from the sky. I hear a muffled Miles' voice praising the Lord from under his downie - rain means I give the boys a lift along the two miles of coastal road to where the school bus collects them. On dry days they cycle.

Miles doesn't mind the cycle ride in itself - it's a beautiful route flanked by beaches and marshlands. By the time they reach the main road the boys have seen a selection of wildlife second to none. Common seals are hauled out, or swimming in the shallows, along the string of wee bays. Curlew, redshank, oystercatcher and other waders (dunlin, sanderling, ringed plover: the list is ongoing) feed along the pebble beaches and wet, coastal fields. Shelduck and lapwing frequent the newly sewn barley fields. Mallard and teal dabble around the long, narrow stone bridge which divides sea from marsh. Shy moorhens vanish along the ditch-lines as the boys-on-bikes approach. A short-eared owl flits silently back and forth across the road, quartering her hunting territory. A raven has taken up residence in our nearest ruin. A merlin watches from a fence post. Skuas and terns fly elegantly overhead, checking out and dodging the resident gulls.

Nearly every day the boys come home with a question. What's the bird with the white-flecked breast/ pointy tail/screechy call? Our bird book is in constant use. Terns are still "comic" (common or arctic). Pipits, finches and larks are still "LBJ's" (little brown jobs). But we're learning. For Miles it's a great chance to gather new stories for his slot in "Word of the Wild", a monthly magazine about the wildlife and natural history of Sanday, written and published by our Secondary One and Two school kids. Affectionately known as WOW, the magazine has been on the go since 1988 and has won awards, many and various, over the years.

In this month's WOW I learn that we have St George's mushrooms forming fairy rings on the schoolhouse lawn, that the mermaid's purses being washed ashore are the egg cases of dogfish, rays and skates (the largest of which are Pacific Ocean fish), that a migrating goldcrest was found in the mouth of a local cat, having been blown off its course to Scandinavia and that an African hoopoe has been seen, having overshot its Mediterranean migrational destination. Starlings' eggs, colourful rabbits, non-breeding herons, pigeon poo, legless toads, lamb quads and ewes with four functional teats - it's fascinating what the kids find to write about. Not that I'm advertising it or anything, but you can get hold of copies via our school.

No, it's not the cycle ride that Miles minds, but the necessity to get out of bed fifteen minutes earlier in order to have time to cycle to the bus. Apparently those fifteen minutes (a whole quarter of an hour, Mum) of extra rest are crucial to his growth and development and I am wrong to deprive him. That's why the drumming of rain on his bedroom window is such a beautiful sound to wake up to.

For me the rain is glorious for another reason. Three days ago the sun shone and the wind dropped to a gentle breeze. The forecast promised rain the following day. Perfect conditions for sowing the lawn seed. Nic and I spent the morning digging up the hundreds of stubborn docken which had sprouted fast from deep within our newly ploughed and rotivated garden. Then we raked and scattered our way across about half an acre of bare earth. By tea-time we were trying to remember the reasoning behind creating such a big garden. Will we ever have time to sit in it? Sunburnt, raw throated and back sore, we finished the job in the gloaming of midnight.

All the next day we scanned an innocently blue sky in vain for that forecast rain. Damnit. The clouds must have blown right on past our wee island and dropped their life giving water on Mainland ground. Yesterday we were blessed with a low mist, which I convinced myself was seeping moisture into the horribly dry looking soil. This morning's rain is real and wet and heavy. Hallelujah.

Swimming ~ *June*

OK, that's enough rain now. The bare earth of our emergent garden has developed an exciting emerald hue - the lawn seed has germinated. I have to admit it's a bit patchy - shall I blame my uneven broadcasting or the vagaries of seed and soil? Either way, we've now had plenty of rain and need some more sunshine and warmth please.

Of all the seasons I find the Orkney spring the most frustrating. Just the fact that June is still referred to as spring should tell you something. While more southerly regions are enjoying heat and sun, water shortages and overgrown gardens, up here we are still wrapping our bodies and our gardens in cosy fleece. Recommended planting dates for flowers and vegetables whiz past us on cruelly cold northerly winds and we must keep our seedlings indoors, turning them daily as they lean to reach the angled light of the window.

My nineteen year old niece is with us this weekend. She was brought up in the South of France and harbours fond memories of long hot summers that seemed to last for three-quarters of each year. But her first winter as a student in Aberdeen has taught her about Scottish temperatures and, nothing daunted, she has already kitted herself out with a wetsuit so that she can jump into the sea whenever the urge takes her. She is aghast to discover that we haven't yet swum from the beach below our fields. In fact we haven't been in Orkney's ocean since last summer. Shamed, we immediately dig out our wetsuits, squeeze our winter flesh into them and off to the beach we go.

Wading through the shallows I realise several things. The water seeping up my legs isn't actually too cold, just refreshing. The view across the sparkling blue waters of Otterswick Bay to the white-blonde sands of Ortie and Saville is stunning. Our schedule of house painting and garden planting has kept us away from beaches for far too long.

With water up to our waists, we take the ultimate plunge and each come up gasping and laughing with the thermal shock of ice-water shrinking our brains. Then we swim out through clear waters, over rock and kelp to a sandy floored area the size of a generous swimming pool. There is something much more relaxing about swimming over sand. I feel a nudge at my shoulder and turn to see Tess, our collie pup. Having diligently followed me this far, she is well out of her depth and tiring. She tries to climb onto me so I give her a lift back to shallower waters then an encouraging shove toward the shore.

When we first appeared over the lip of the beach the resident common seals flipped into the sea from their haul out at the far end of the bay. Now heads bob up all around us and as always my awe at their proximity mingles with apprehension. How close will they come? Do our black suits make us look like intruding sea mammals? Will their inquisitiveness ever turn to aggression? Those big bull seals are a helluva size when seen from a mere five yards away. Certainly bigger than an eight-year-old boy, for instance.

My fears are unfounded. The seals dip and dive and surface and roll onto their backs. They seem to want to play. When we wade ashore and towel off they are still there, watching mutely. Back at home I check my email and find four fabulous photos sent by my friends on Orkney Mainland. On a boat trip off the Dearness coast they came across a pod of six Orca (Killer whales). One shot shows the hugeness of the whales in contrast to a tiny round head - a seal, looking as vulnerable as a small child. The legend refers to the seal in the past tense. RIP.

This week's Orcadian newspaper also sports a sea mammal photograph. A school of common dolphins have been seen fishing around the first Churchill Barrier. Over the past year I have heard many stories of sea mammal sightings, from the Humpbacked whales of last autumn to orcas, dolphins and porpoises. Now that summer is finally upon us I think its time I got out more, whether with wetsuit and windsurfer or on ferries to other islands, and set my sights on some sea-watching.

Picnic day ~ *June*

This is picnic day. I don't mean any old picnic. This is our island community's traditional annual picnic, when everyone gets together on our much used playing fields to enjoy a day of fun in the sun. And mostly (touch wood) by the luck of Fate or some Guardian Angel watching over us, the annual Sanday Picnic Day does seem to land on a sunny day.

For us punters the day starts at a civilized 1pm, but we can tell from the state of the field that the stalwart army of volunteer organizers have put in many hours of preparation. Before we can explore the rows of stalls we are magnetically drawn to a gathering crowd of folk at the edge of the running track. They are watching and laughing and applauding someone in their midst. It's Malcolm Russell, self-professed magician and physical comic, out from Kirkwall to do a few magic shows for us islanders. We settle down on the grass to watch as he intersperses puzzling card tricks with ridiculous balancing acts: a trestle table balanced vertically on his chin, for instance. In a force four breeze that's pretty whacky.

Dispersing from the magic ring we take a look around the side shows. Trick cycles (with wobbly wheels), "Aiming in the tyres", "Penalty Shoot Out", "Milking the Coo", "Target Gold" and the ubiquitous "Wellie Chuck". Miles excels himself at the "Hoops and Quoits" and wins two coconuts at the Shy. My talent turns out to be at "Splat the Rat" - a wriggling brown whiskery sock released down a drain pipe that you have to swipe with a cricket bat it as it emerges from the other end. Sounds simple? - do try it at home.

Dale and Fenning have their antennae out for one promised and much discussed treat and vanish from our sights as soon as it appears. The candy floss stall, in a Punch-and-Judy red tent, sports a raggedy line of increasingly sticky children for the rest of the afternoon. Fuelled with the pink spun sugar, they all head for the bouncy castle: a recipe for disaster one would imagine, but kids have incredibly resilient digestive systems.

Round the edge of the field are some bizarre constructs and Nic and I size them up with a degree of apprehension. This is the "Beat the Clock" team event - a latter day "It's a Knockout" and Nic, Miles and I have all been volunteered on to teams. By three o'clock we are all rounded up - six teams, each consisting of eight people, a male and a female each from four age ranges (I am outraged to discover I'm in the oldest age range: where are all the fit over fifty's?) - and the school gym teacher is bawling instructions at us in her town-crier voice.

As you can imagine if you ever watched It's a Knockout, the next hour and a half involves balloons, water, balancing bars, slippery slopes, more water, washing-up-liquid, magnetic fishing rods and yet more water. We play three-legged football, race on bouncy-hoppers and blast each other with super-soakers. All good clean fun and not too many injuries.

A change of clothes then it's time for tea - the usual islander spread of trestle tables laden with home-baked delectables. By 5pm the wind is up and the sun has gone and we're all a bit weary for the football and netball matches still to come. But as the referees blow their starting whistles and the balls fly on all four pitches, so the clouds give way to blue sky, a warm evening sun emerges, the wind drops and the sea sparkles once more.

Financed by the incredible fund-raising skills of the community and run entirely by volunteers, this whole day of fun and food has been free of charge. It's great not to have to dig in your pockets every time your child wants another go at the coconuts or another bounce on the castle. And it's not over yet. There's just time to pop home for yet another change of clothing before the evening's entertainment of music and dancing in the hall, with a prize-giving, supper, another fantastical magic show and the last waltz at 2am. Remote island life: never a dull moment.

Jazz ~ July

If I were to honestly write about the dominant activity of our week then this column would reek of blocked pipes, overflowing drains and a mysterious amount of broken glass in the septic tank. There is certainly enough material in the ins and outs, the ups and downs, the stops and the go's of an old house's plumbing system to fill a small book. In fact we were wondering, by Friday, why, when one buys something like a car one gets an in depth manual with handy diagrams of how everything sticks together and functions, yet with the purchase of a house there is no such thing. Why don't the house title deeds come with a map of plumbing, electricity and phone line routes?

But that would be a horrid subject, so I'll move swiftly on.

Last week saw the start of the St Magnus Festival, Orkney's annual, internationally renowned, stramash of music, art and performance. Most of the events take place in Kirkwall and Stromness but each year a selection of the world class performers who take part are sent "on tour". For them Orkney Mainland is already far from home so travelling out to Stronsay, Westray, Sanday or Hoy must be deemed an outlandish tour within a tour.

This year Sanday was treated to an opening night performance by the Grand Union Scottish Band. As is now traditional, the musicians arrived in the morning and spent the day holding workshops for our school kids. The boys came home wreathed in smiles - they'd had a great time. We were treated to their interpretations of South African vocals, a weird Chinese stringy thing in a box, a variety of drumming techniques and the delightful notion of making music through shaking and thumping things (the popcorn jar in this case). Above all it seemed to me that they had learnt about rhythm, listening to a musical phrase and responding to it: they'd learnt about musical improvisation.

We go along to the evening performance intrigued to see all the strange instruments the boys have described. As usual we're within a whisker of lateness and have to squeeze in to a packed, hot school hall. Everyone's chatting away, catching up, fetching drinks from the trestle table bar at the back, when a lone, deep and powerful voice stops us in our tracks. The other seven musicians sing a response, the lone voice sings again, the others respond and suddenly I'm transported back to my travels through Africa when I heard this spontaneous singing from street corners, fields, the back of trucks - everywhere.

With the audience suitably spellbound the concert begins. The stage is a riot of instruments and musicians. I count at least twenty instruments: saxophones (soprano, baritone and tenor), flute, fiddle, trombone, base guitar, drums (tabla, conga and what I'd call a normal drumkit), keyboards, harp, maracas, melodica and referee's whistle to name but a few. The weird Chinese box turns out to be a yangqin - a dulcimer, if that helps explain it better - which can make the most wonderful range of noises. Another strange box holds a marimbol - described to me after the show as sort of like a thumb piano. My favourite, possibly because it only has two strings and looks relatively easy to play, is the erhu - the Chinese fiddle.

The musicians are an equally eclectic mix: Scottish, Chinese, Bangladeshi, South African, English, Australian, Mexican. The pieces are ingenious mosaics of Gaelic, Celtic, Latin and Oriental origin. After a brief interval the kids are lined up to do their thing with fiddles, recorders, thumpey things and shakey things. Then we're treated to another hour of awe inspiring, foot tapping, body jiggling music.

As the musicians dismantle and pack away their instruments curiosity gets the better of me so I go up and ask what everything is called. The boys get to thump the drums and finger the keyboards. Before we leave we're even shown how to drain spit out of a melodica. But don't let me get back on to the subject of drains.

Garden ~ *July*

Last night, in the late, fading sunlight of our Orkney simmer dim, Nic gave our lawn it's first ever haircut. The patchy swathe of bright green tufts went from a raggedy three inches to a uniform one and a half inches and from babyhood to all grown up. By the time the job was finished I was so fixated on my "baby's first haircut" analogy that I almost scooped up a handful of grass cuttings to save in a pot for posterity. I am, as you may have noticed, a tad excited about creating our own garden from scratch.

I am also creating the garden the wrong way round. In my haste and enthusiasm I've already planted a central triangle of herbs. Parsley, sage (not rosemary) and thyme are all growing and thriving in our sandy soil, alongside chamomile, oregano, marjoram, blue hyssop, chives, sorrel, angelica and several varieties of mint. In the veggie plot I have over three hundred tattie plants emerging and a few wee rows of carrots, lettuce, rocket and coriander still deciding if it's warm enough to germinate. Around our electricity pylon, which rudely interrupts the aesthetics of our garden, I have planted a half moon of many-times-split rhubarb hearts.

With some small amount of guilt (I'm fairly sure one is not supposed to remove plants from a property one has just sold) I have retrieved my dozen Valentine's Day rose bushes from the old garden and planted those along the other side of an as yet imaginary path. They look slightly shocked at this untimely transplant, but I have bedded them down in nice deep trenches lined with top quality two-year-old horse manure (thanks Chuck), so I think they'll pull through. I have taken copious willow cuttings (with less guilt because the willow desperately needed a trim) and am nursing them along in buckets of water. We have, as you know, sown the lawn.

The missing bit, the place I should have started, is the perimeter hedge. Shelter from the wind is paramount to garden success up here, especially where we are - within half a mile of the coast. Do my hastily planted herbs stand a chance of surviving the salt-laden gales without a hardy hedge to protect them? In my defence I have made all the right moves toward hedging.

The initial ploughing and rotivation of the field resulted in a handy trench around the garden, just inside the new stock-proof fence. I have allowed for about six foot of space between the fence and the lawn, for two, staggered, rows of hedging plants to grow and thicken into the desired windbreak. I've even drawn up a plan of where all the curves of paths and stretches of herbaceous borders and occasional ornamental tree-ettes will live.

The reason for the lack of actual hedge is that it's just not the right time to plant one. I could buy in ready grown bushes now, at vast cost, or I could listen to every piece of hedging advice offered so far and buy root stock in the fall, at a fraction of that cost, for planting in early spring. It's not like me to listen to reason when it gets in the way of speed, but when it affects my purse too, well that's different.

I have had fun delving in to plant and gardening books to decide what species to use for my hedge. The list of heroic species that can withstand and thrive in Orkney's maritime climate - salt-laden winds, stormy weather, a short growing season and a coolish one at that - is surprisingly long. Sea-buckthorn, hawthorn, hornbeam, willow, escallonia, flowering current, elder, gorse, fuchsia, gooseberry, dog rose, hazel and downy birch are all on my list.

While we await the arrival of hundreds of local provenance root stock we won't be idle. We have to deepen and widen the trench and layer it with enriching substances - probably manure and seaweed - to give our hedge the best possible start in life.

Harvest ~ *July*

I talk about the weather a lot these days. It may be that, aged forty-something, I have finally stopped railing against that peculiar, eccentric British tradition. Or perhaps I've got caught up in what is a particular Orkney obsession: I would estimate that 90% of conversations here open with a weather comment. "A fine day, aye." "a peedie bit weet" "fairly blowin'".

There is one that I love, for its wonderful Orcadian optimism - "Aye, but I doot it'll be better the morn'" (Orcadians use the word doubt in its positive form ie they mean "I do think" rather than "I don't think"). I was extra delighted when eight-year-old Dale came out with it yesterday, while he and I were cycling through the rain to his basketball summer-school class. Everlasting optimism in the face of adversity is catching.

Of course the more sobering reason for all our weather talk is that it can make or break the success of the farming year. During Orkney's short growing season a winter's worth of animal feed is grown, harvested and stored. Through a very wet June I watched as grass destined to become hay or silage grew long and fell over under the weight of water and the force of the wind. Barley crops, each with their traditional strip of tatties and greens alongside, fared better as they were still short enough to put up with the battering.

In every tiny weather window from mid-June on, tractors appeared all over the island to quickly cut or turn or gather in the silage. Their synchronicity was such that we wondered if the farmers all phoned each other to discuss the right moment to harvest a crop, but we concluded that it's more likely that, with many generations of farming in their genes, they can feel it in their bones.

With the silage safely in and stored either in large pits or wrapped in round green or black plastic "dougals" it's time to look at the hay fields. For the many farmers who have signed up to conservation initiatives, there is the added stress of awaiting a cutting date of mid-July or even the first of August. This gives our rare corncrakes and other ground nesting waders time to raise their broods and for their long-legged chicks to scarper when they hear the sound of tractors.

The most commonly grown grain here is barley. Bere, the primitive six-rowed variety of barley, has been grown in Orkney for thousands of years. Planted in April or May and herbicided and rolled when a tender two to three inches long, half-grown barley fields all over the island are now more than a foot deep in their neon-bright green swards. This fodder crop is traditionally harvested in September and packed away in dry barn pits with a nasty acidic preservative nick-named "prop-corn", to be bruised and fed to the cattle as required through the winter.

Yesterday I was shown the modern crimping method, which seems to have two great advantages. The barley is harvested earlier - in August - and the crimping machine squashes the otherwise inedible corns and applies crimp-store preservative all in one go. The resultant ready-to-eat feed is packed like silage and cut in to when needed. Fast food for cows.

Our July weather is mostly looking better than cold, wet, unpredictable June. But last weekend saw a bizarre phenomenon. While we north-enders enjoyed sun and dry skies, the south end of this 15mile long island had thunder, lightening and enough rain to flood the roads and several houses. This prompted memories of lightening strikes (and on this flat island there have been many) lifting the roofs off houses, killing cows, turning the electricity wires red-hot and zapping the local sub-station. The classic sign of an impending electrical thunder storm is apparently steam rising off the roads. Some sort of temperature inversion I suppose, but I haven't quite got to grips with that story yet.

Pots ~ *July*

A couple of months ago I was volunteered into running a pottery day as part of the summer-school activities for our island school children.

At this point I'd like to explain the concept of volunteering within small island communities. The process whereby one ends up doing something for no remuneration, out of the goodness of one's heart, for the greater good of the community, is very straightforward. One is asked, eyeball to eyeball, by the person or committee who is running that particular project, usually also on a voluntary basis. The collective island eyes and ears tune in to catch your response and to make you squirm and that heady mix of dread, guilt and the desire to please kicks in. You have been got. The metaphorical arm being gently turned and held behind your back really has nothing to do with it - I wouldn't call it coercion at all. But one is definitely "volunteered" rather than choosing to "volunteer".

Anyway, I digress. This morning at 8am finds me loading the landrover with props - clay cutting and modelling tools, some instruction sheets I prepared earlier (well, Nic did it for me last night actually), pottery books and some examples of bowls, egg cups candlesticks and plates - the inhabitants of our kitchen dresser. Running through my mind are the predictable themes: why did I agree to this, I've never done any teaching, my potting methods are unorthodox (I make it up as I go along), I'd rather be out in my garden etc etc.

By 9am, with the help of our summer school organiser, I'm all set up in the school art room. Twelve eight to ten year olds are duly delivered. About half have remembered pinnies and we kit the rest out from the domestic science store. I'm pleased to see an even mix of girls and boys - I had feared that this would be perceived as a girly activity, but the kids brought up here seem mercifully free of such notions.

My introductory talk, which kept me awake for most of last night, turns into a rapidly garbled spiel about the origins of clay - what is it, where does it come from, how come it's so versatile - bluntly interrupted by, "can we have the clay now, please" from several of the keenest participants. I drag dim memories of art class from my school days and arrange the children in pairs, each sharing a table and an instruction sheet. We hand out twelve modelling boards and lumps of grey clay. I quickly explain the rudiments of the pinch and coil pottery-making methods. The kids watch and listen politely, but their faces are a strain of impatience, their hands twitch to get stuck in.

By 10am we have the most amazing array of pots, from a girl with many siblings who has divided her clay ball accordingly and made a carefully coiled eggcup for each, to a boy with a big appetite who has used up all his clay in one go to make one huge cereal bowl. They announce that they have finished. Panic rises within me: the class is supposed to continue until midday. For the next half hour I teach them to check their pots for flaws - is the base firmly stuck to the walls, are there any gaps between the coils, is the rim smooth, are the walls sagging, have they marked their pots with their initials?

10.30am. The classroom is hot. The sun is shining. The view from the windows takes in the swings and slides of the playground, farm fields and a sparkling ocean beyond. We decide that half an hour of playtime is in order.

The break does us all a power of good. There's a girl whose clay is a battered flat pancake on the table. I'm at a loss as to what to do with it, but she comes back in at 11am, peels her clay off the table, wraps it into a cylindrical shape, sticks it to a small disc of clay and bingo, she's made a vase. Everyone else has thought of some alteration or addition to their pots. By noon we have the finished pieces all lined up to dry before their firing, we have clean tables, clean hands and a drawing from each child depicting the colours they envisage for their pots - there's a glazing session in two weeks. Phew - I think it all went OK. And the positive aspect of being volunteered into this? To my surprise, I have enjoyed it.

Shearing 1 ~ *July*

Sheep farming, lesson three: shearing. Or clipping. It's equally difficult whatever you call it. But we have five very shaggy Jacob sheep and the job needs doing. "Clip sheep" has been chalked onto our kitchen blackboard for about a month now, but with no gear and no know-how, we've been averting our gaze from the accusing words hoping for some solution to present itself. '

Last weekend it did. Our farming friends from Westray, who sold us our wee collie, Tess, were coming over on the Sunday excursion trip. Throughout the summer months Orkney Ferries lay on a direct, Sunday service between pairs of islands, allowing for day trips without the need to land on Orkney Mainland. Last Sunday the timetable allowed for Westray folk to visit Sanday.

Now Marcus and Barbara keep, to my knowledge, 900 ewes, and they had been telling us tales of a team of five folk shearing 600 in a day. To my mind that meant that Marcus alone could do our five in about five minutes. I invited them to share our Sunday dinner and teach us to clip our sheep between courses. The deal was struck. All we had to do was cook up a feast and get the sheep under cover for the night to ensure that their fleeces were dry.

To dyed-in-the-wool farmers, getting a bunch of sheep off a six acre field and into a small byre is the work of a moment. To us it's an operation requiring military style planning plus a small army of boys and dogs. But now I have discovered a secret weapon which renders the task a whole lot easier. For the past two months we have been putting sheep nuts out in the yard and leaving the gate open - result, tame sheep. With the yard gate swung shut behind them, all we had to do was lure them into the byre. Again the feed tin proved handy and, with the dogs sniffing at their heels, we had the flock inside in a jiffy (well, about half an hour actually, but it was a whole heap easier than we feared).

Orkney rib-roast, tatties, yorkies, carrots, beans and gravy. Barbara brings sweeties and a coin for each of the boys, a fine selection of Westray breads and a Westray display plate for our dresser. Marcus inspects every inch of our wee farm and announces it "dead right" "a grand set up" and "very fine indeed".

Then it's down to the business of setting up the clipping rig in the byre, sweeping a clean space and bringing out the first victim. Marcus holds the ewe easily between his legs and does the first clipping at full pace, just to let us see how easy it is. Divide the fleece up her neck and flip it over her head, then clip down the belly, round the teats, over the back left leg, up the left side, across the back of the neck, down the right side and finish at the top of her tail. Within a minute there's a complete fleece lying on the ground and a shorn, goat-like, bewildered sheep released out to the yard. What could be easier?

With the second ewe Marcus slows right down and gives us the step-by-step guide. It's like a slow dance as he moves round the sheep, holding her secure yet accessing successive parts of her body and keeping the clippers snug between wool and skin all the while. He admits he doesn't like working with horned sheep - with their head between your legs it can be a tricky business. He shows me how to gather up the fleece, fling it out onto clean ground then fold and roll it tightly. The wool is surprisingly thick, almost like felt, and luxuriously soft. My hands slip with wool-oil and reek of lanolin.

With ewes three, four and five the lesson is repeated and Nic has a go with the clippers. Aha - it's not as easy as it looks. We are clearly not going to learn this life-skill in one afternoon. A plan is hatched - we'll go to Westray next June to help with his clipping then he'll come here and help with ours. Despite the difference in flock size, I think we have the better end of the deal.

Old hay ~ *August*

The ageing process is not pretty, not clever. For my 42nd birthday I wake up with a cricked shoulder, blistered hands and all over muscle ache. OK so we spent yesterday humphing about 600 old hay bales out of the sheep byre, but there were six of us and everyone else (average age 15) still looks bouncy and supple.

When we moved to this wee farm back in May the two old byres were stuffed - floor to ceiling - with hay bales. Our hens, cats, kittens (there were four in the end), dogs and children loved it. The hens laid their eggs all over the place and could climb up to the highest rafters to roost. The dogs could chase the cats, safe in the knowledge that they would never actually get close enough to have to enact the pretence of ferocity. The boys could climb up to the hay loft and launch themselves off again into a soft sea of hay.

For us groans (boring grown ups, in case you haven't come across the expression) the inevitable need to clear all the hay out was a daunting prospect. I knew we'd have to do it before this year's hay crop was brought in so, when the tractors arrived to cut our grass fields last week, it was "game on" and all hands to the binder twine, so to speak.

Clever twelve-year-old Miles put his thinking cap on and came up with a new cliché - a work-load shared is a work-load halved. He invited a friend over. As they are both raising funds for a school trip to France next February, we gave them the extra incentive of a wage and this, combined with an element of competitive muscle prowess (look at me, I can carry two bales at once), egged them on to impressive amounts of work.

At eight, Dale and a damp old bale of hay are probably about the same weight. He wrestled a few out of the door and a few more wrestled him to the ground before we decided he was better off using a wheelbarrow for the job. Seven-year-old Fenning (his birthday was last week and involved so much boy-noise and mess that I haven't the energy to write about it) had no intention of involving himself directly with a bale of hay, but picked up the yard broom and did a lot of useful sweeping.

Fenning was also our egg-spert - a job a bit like bomb disposal. Whenever any of us found old hen's eggs among the bales he would carry them carefully down the beach track and throw them as far as possible along the ditch whence they exploded with a loud pop and disgorged their putrid contents. At one point, to my horror, I unearthed a long-dead hen (not one of ours) still sitting on a dozen eggs. Did she just die on the job, of old age, or should we suspect foul play? We found a good number of dead rats into the bargain.

The best bit was when we all collapsed on to the last few bales with a beer (or a coke for the child labourers) and admired our cleared byre. We could now properly see the old stone walls and wooden rafters, the underside of the heavily slated roof and the row of sixteen traditional cow stalls divided by huge slabs of vertical flagstone, each with its own water trough and a chain for the cow. The boys grabbed their bikes and cycled up and down the central gutter, out through the back door, round the track and back in through the yard. We declared the byre ready to receive new hay and went in for tea.

Last week my green-fingered mother-in-law brought, and planted out, numerous garden plants for me. Potentilla, escallonia, hebe, dogwood, roses, hydrangea, buddleia and berberis shrubs now adorn the new herbaceous borders. She even brought me six tree saplings - maple, oak and horse chestnut. In my fear for their survival I have sheltered each with a coralle of, you guessed it, hay bales. My other birthday presies from the boys include two garden bench seats and a styled-for-comfort linen outfit - they really are putting me out to grass.

Shells - *August*

This low-lying, sprawling Orkney island isn't called Sanday for nothing. If you ran the 60 miles of its coastline then you'd be running on sand, the theme tune to Chariots of Fire ringing in your head, for 27 of those miles - almost 50% of your journey. This is, I hasten to add, a rough measurement with a piece of string and a map. Running the coastline is one of my too-far-down-the-priority-list desires that might happen within the next decade. And I'll probably be walking. Or maybe riding a horse.

Some of the beaches are shingle, some strewn with a tide line of kelp and the flotsam and jetsam of ocean life. But mostly you'll have the gritty texture of pure shell sand beneath your feet, massaging you soles and edging between your toes. That's assuming that, like me, you can't resist taking off your boots whenever you hit a beach.

Tides, temperature and wave action are all important in determining the abundance and distribution of inshore marine mollusc species - the makers and inhabitants of all those shells. Neither Orkney's air nor sea temperatures vary much with season, which gives these heat and light sensitive animals a good survival rate. The most problematic climatic threat for them here is the wind - they are prone to desiccation when exposed at low tide. But their death and the relentless pounding of the waves on their empty shells produces its own abundance - of shell sand - around our coasts.

Miles upon miles of, usually deserted, sandy beaches are fantastic things to live beside. The stuff of childhood, summer holiday memories. A place to stretch your limbs and gather your thoughts, with nothing but the wind and a far off fishing boat for company. Nothing but the dip of a seal and the rise and fall of a flock of foraging waders to disturb your silence. My niece was doing just that, down on our beach, while she waited for her university exam results a few weeks ago.

She came back up to the house curving the hem of her jumper up into a pouch brimming with wee shells. Spilled out onto the kitchen table they became a mini-beach, a slew of colour with a whiff of salt tang to please our senses. She had almost exclusively chosen periwinkles ("buckies" in Orcadian-speak). Their smooth shells radiated shades of yellow, red, orange and green from their dark wood background. Armed with a fine drill she set about selecting stripey then plain, grooved then smooth, bold then delicate shells to bore a hole through and feed along a thread. By tea-time she had a fine necklace to take home.

Among her pile, rejected for the necklace because of their differing sizes, were a few other shell types. They reminded me of a Sanday wedding last summer. I walked past the Community Hall window one day and saw that it was all decked out in wedding finery, ready for a feast that evening. Taped to the window was the seating plan, which I read with delight. For each table had been given the name of a local shell. Faeroe sunset shell, groatie buckie (cowrie), painted topshell, spoot (razor shell), cockle, scallop, periwinkle, whelk, common limpet, tellin (butterfly shell) and tower shell. Was each table decorated with the shell of its name, gathered from our local beaches? I peered through the windows, but couldn't see the tables well enough. And did the guests go home with a shell each?

My favourite shell has always been the cowrie. The way its fine grooves curve quietly round and tuck in on themselves fascinates me. When I was six we took a family holiday on Tiree and I gathered pockets full of them. I now have a big jug of all those shells, which has to be carefully wrapped and packed every time I move house. I haven't worked out why, given the cowrie's delicate pinkish colour and petite prettiness, it should be dubbed a "groatie buckie" by Orcadians. For once the dialect seems to have failed in its usually vivid descriptive abilities. On the other hand their "scadman's heid" for sea urchin is spectacularly descriptive for those spikey, dishevelled heads and one of my favourite nicknames - though I don't always use it to refer to a shell.

Sooth - *August*

Our hay fields were cut just before we headed "Sooth" for a week and I must admit that I have never felt less like leaving home. To anyone not involved in farming or keeping horses, this may seem a tad eccentric, but the thing is that once the grass is cut you really want to watch over it until it is safely stacked in your byre for the winter.

For a few days we watched helplessly as our mixed Orkney summer weather first dried then soaked the lines of felled grass. With clever machinery the grass was flipped and spread out to dry, then collected back into lines ready for baling. At the start of what promised to be a good week of sun the baler arrived and we watched, fascinated, as the tractor trundled up and down spewing out square bales to a man perched on the back stacking them onto a four pronged trailer. Four bales along the base, three on top of them, two on the next layer and finally a single bale to complete the pyramid. At this point the tractor would lower the trailer to deposit this variant on the hay stook and thence continue gathering and baling and twining the next row of hay.

In the dusky warmth of evening we walked around the stooks inhaling the gorgeous sweet, fresh herbiness of our hay. A couple more days of sun and it would be perfectly dry for storing. But next afternoon we headed south through mizzle (misty drizzle) with sinking hearts. The hay would be getting wetter, not drier.

To cheer me up the boys devised a daily treat programme, the first of which was a trip to Thurso's cinema to see "Shrek 2". The list continued with "Spiderman 2" and "Thunderbirds", a day in a rollercoaster theme park and finally a shopping trip to an electronics store (Gameboy games and DVD's featured highly in their chatter on the road south): perhaps not tailor-made for me, but their intentions were pure.

While Nic negotiated the hairpin fall and rise of the Berriedale Braes through thick mist, I received a call from our animal sitter. The dogs were fine but the hens were eating the cat food, the cats had vanished and the lambs were playing "king of the castle" on the hay stooks. And a monstrous beast had just been delivered into the back field. My heart sank another notch - our latest animal purchase had arrived and I wasn't even there to greet her. OK. This called for some emergency measures of stoicism and positive thinking. Our week was action packed with visits to relatives and friends, shopping and the above mentioned "treats". I might as well enjoy it.

Sure enough the week has passed in a whirl of seeing loved ones, socialising, traffic jams, crowds and parting with money and before we know it here we are back on the good old A9 driving through Scotland.
North of Inverness the mist engulfs us. Has it been misty all week up here? At Latheronwheel we turn inland, cutting off the north-eastern tip of Scotland for the final leg to Thurso. The narrower road wends its way through thick swathes of mist. Just south of Spittal some twenty or more wind turbines loom above us, swinging their arms like great Frankensteinian monsters, stark white torsos dwarfing a small plantation of Sitka spruce trees on the barren hillside. An exciting Scottish industry of the future symbolically dwarfing one of the past. This is the Causeymire Wind Farm, beautiful, to me, in its simple, visual gathering of a natural and plentiful source of power.

At last we are going the right way across the Pentland Firth (am I becoming a tad xenophobic?). The ship's fog horn booms through great rolling blankets of haar. Then the sea mist miraculously lifts to reveal a stunning vista of the green-gold folds of the cliffs of Hoy, the Old Man standing proud sentinel in the foreground. As soon as we've passed St. John's Head the haar engulfs us once more and the rest of our journey home is through a thick fog of white.

As our engine dies outside our house we can hear the thunder of giant hooves through the mist. A massive dark bulk appears at the field gate and snorts a wary greeting. The newest member of our family of animals is Lady Helen: not so much a monster as a great big beautiful Clydesdale horse.

County show ~ *August*

The mist is clearing to the promise of a fine morning. We're up and out early, feeding animals, releasing them from their night roosts, checking their water supplies, giving the dogs a run to the beach, preparing them for a long day without us.

By 07.15am we're on our way, rumbling along our recently smoothed track, enjoying the temporary lack of pot-holes. Through a yet sleeping Lady Village Miles' friend waits at the roadside for us to pick him up. Jeans, trainers, t-shirt and a grin of excitement. No jumper, no jacket, no bag - he travels light, this boy.

As we drive the long, dog-legged, South-end road to Loth and a waiting ferry, I wish for a bird's eye view of Orkney. I imagine the spider's web of her roads alive with the specks of cars and lorries, tractors and trailers, all converging on one field. Bignold Park, Kirkwall is the site of Orkney Agricultural Society's 118th County Show.

Our ferry is direct and swift this morning: we're in Kirkwall by 09.30am. But even at that, by the time we get up the road to the showground we've missed a good deal of the livestock judging, which started at 08.30am. The entrance gates are bristling with officials and there's a tense moment as someone tries to enter the grounds without stopping at the ticket booth. Laid-back, crime-free Orkney isn't used to such bold cheek.

Inside the gates the boys are immediately pulling in different directions: a booth stacked with toy tractors and weird fluffy snakes to our right, a rank of brand new quad bikes to our left, a flight simulator right in front of us. But, through the crowds up ahead I have spied a ring with some large and beautiful horses. Nic quickly scans the programme of events: we're just in time to watch the Clydesdale classes being judged. For once I am deaf to the cries of boys' desires as I forge ahead through sauntering families, straggling toddlers and leashed dogs to reach the ringside.

After a good dose of horse admiring it is time to indulge the boys and we've seen Kirby, our favourite beefburger stall, at the other side of the main ring. We send the twelve-year-olds ahead to stand in the straggling queue while we take a look at the cattle. From Shorthorn to Charolais, Ayrshire to Aberdeen Angus, Native breeds to Continentals, they are lined up, groomed and glossy. The cattle judging ring itself is hard to see, surrounded as it is by serious-faced farmers, dressed in their best and deep in debate as each beast is led in and round.

Miles texts us to say they are two from the front of the food queue: time for us to get there. When we do we can hardly hear ourselves think for the madly loud pop music blasting forth from the main ring's loudspeakers. There's something strange going on in there and the crowds are a dozen deep to see what it is. A woman dancing with her dogs, as it turns out. Whatever next?

After a tasty munch of Orkney's finest beef, we continue round the showpark to the sheep pens for a good look at all those different breeds. The boys drag behind us, bored, while we study the Suffolk and Texel entrants. But the big hare-like ears and noble noses of the Border Leicesters catch their attention and thereafter the four of them skip round the pens playing guess-the-breed and the more tricky game of guess-the-cross-breed.

Two things left on our list. First a good scrutiny of the lovely new tractors on display - would we buy blue, red or green if we could afford these luxurious giants at all? - and an oggle at all the farm machinery - ploughs, mowers, harvesters, brush cutters, seeders, spreaders - trying to guess what everything does. Second the boys need to blow off some more energy on one of the showground helter-skelters across the road. Then it's time to scarper, leave the heat, bustle and noise of the show and head off to our friends' house for tea before the evening boat home.

⌐

Red sky in the morning

~ Autumn 2004

Triathlon ~ *August*

I'm not a great fan of the sponsored activity as a way of raising funds for personal use. I can still remember taking part in a twenty mile sponsored bed-push (how mad was that?) when I was in my early teens. I can't remember what we were raising money for, but I distinctly recall the pain of asking perfectly innocent, decent neighbours and friends-of-my-parents to promise me an amount per mile completed. And the excruciating embarrassment of having to call on them again to extract the monies from their reluctant hands also lives on in my childhood memory bank.

So when twelve-year-old Miles hatched a plan to do a sponsored "something" in order to raise money for his school trip to France next February, I have to admit to a flicker of dismay. But then, there's only so much money to be earned through washing cars, clearing hay byres and weeding gardens and with twenty-six school kids trying to raise funds on the island, I did think that Miles' idea to tap some off-island sources was pretty sound. Plus it gave us a new focus, just as the summer holidays were edging into boredom.

With a head full of Olympian images Miles decided to undertake a triathlon. He planned to begin with a run from our tall, stripey lighthouse at Start Point, then cycle the length of our island - roughly twenty miles from north-east to south-west, stopping on the way for a swim. He was tempted by an open water swim, but what with our famous British summer weather this year, the ocean looked a tad chilly. We booked the community swimming pool.

Miles sent off explanatory maps to distant relatives and urban friends and Nic studied the tide tables (the lighthouse being on a tidal island) and phoned the Start Point landowner. We settled on the last day of the holidays for our adventure. The tide was low for an early start and the weather - well we'd just have to take what came.

The day dawned dry and clear, wisps of white cotton cloud teased across blue skies. At 6am we set off for the North-end with three sleepy boys, two bouncing dogs, two bikes, swimming gear and a picnic. Nic and Miles took on the running leg across Ayre Sound to the Lighthouse and back while I got the bikes out. Twenty minutes later Dale and I jogged through the cool early morning air to watch the runners return, skipping over boulders, sliding over kelp-strewn shingle, jumping rock-pools as they made their way back across the causeway. The tide had turned, but hadn't flooded the Sound yet. At the boat-house we high-fived to a successful first phase and laughed at our clouds of hot breath in the cold air.

Phase two. Miles and I set off on our bikes for the long road to the centre of this island. We bumped along the sand track round the southern edge of Scuthvie Bay, a herring gull screeching protest at our intrusion. Then we were on tarmac and heading through the ripening barley and cut hay fields of Northwall, Rusness and Sellibister, the sand dunes of Lopness Bay to our left, the wind and sun behind us all the way. After Newark we free-wheeled across the open, windy expanse of the Plain of Fidge, surprising some early morning golfers and a hunting Short-eared owl. At the edge of Lady Village we paused to gulp water and stare across the vast beauty of Cata Sands, slews of wading birds feeding round the edge of the tidal basin.

At the pool Nic and I lifeguarded while Miles did his twenty lengths. We threw Dale and Fenning in too, for a quick wake up swim. After the fresh air of the great outdoors, being inside felt stuffy and hot and claustrophobic. Fortified by a picnic breakfast it was down to Miles and Nic to cycle the final leg down to Loth. Eight miles and a few hills: I challenged them to get there in an hour. Forty-five minutes later they came whizzing and whooping down the hill to the pier. An easy ride, they said, despite dodging cows on the road and stopping to take in the panoramic views across the sparkling sea of Sanday Sound to our neighbouring islands, Stronsay and Eday. Phew. On the strength of our triathlon exertions we have since enjoyed two weeks of watching the Olympics on TV, in the guilt-free knowledge that we're not just armchair enthusiasts.

Leemill ~ *September*

My, but it's been a wee bit blowy this week. Or, rather, it has been a week of contrasts. One day we were lolling in the heat of the afternoon, shading our eyes from the intense sun as we drowsily chatted with friends around our garden table while the boys played "who can get wettest" with the garden hose. Next day said garden table blew over (and it's not light) with the help of 60 mile per hour winds.

The week continued with squalls of wind and rain interspersed with flashes of sunshine and moments of calm. It was a useful week for us to find out more about our new farm before the winter sets in. We have discovered which of the byre doors flap and which are solid, which windows rattle and which, as it happened, break entirely and need to be replaced. We now know for sure that our outdoor trampoline is going to have to be guy-roped down and we have discovered to our delight that the main yard, walled in, as it is, on three sides by sheep byre, stables and workshop, is a haven of shelter in anything but a north-easterly. I'm already drawing up plans for a building on that fourth side.

With the handy foresight offered to us via the "Farmers Weekly" weather texts, we knew this wind was on its way. To protect our garden we spent that last calm evening rolling out yard after yard of close-knit green netting and battening it to the fence. Feeling like some fishwife mending her nets I endlessly laced the flimsy edge of green to the top-wire of stock-fence. The blurb on the packaging suggested that this fencing would reduce airflow by 50% and protect delicate plants from gale force winds.

Well, I can't complain on that score - our garden plants are still standing proud (unlike the barley crop across the track, which is sadly battered and flattened). What we didn't reckon on was that the force of the wind hitting such a barrier could (did, actually) uproot the whole structure of the fence, which now leans at a jaunty angle, the stabs swivelling freely in their holes. More work needed.

Before the gales hit we had a visitor and, in time honoured fashion, put him to work. Ages ago we bought a wee windmill. Now, with all the little extras - nine metre metal pole, metal guy ropes, heavy-duty bolt tensioners, deep-cycle batteries, inverter, concrete blocks and masonry drill - sourced, a site figured out and a techy friend to help, Nic was ready to put it up. All day long I watched from my desk as they to'd and fro'd carrying windmill parts, tools, instruction sheets and beer cans between workshop and site. I would have offered to help but I could see it was one of those "men are from Mars" projects. Twice I had to wheel out the first-aid kit as one then the other (do they never learn?) smashed his hand between a rock and a hard place. As the afternoon progressed the weather turned from mild and sunny to blustery and very, very wet.

Undeterred (i.e. bloody determined not to quit) they laboured on into the evening. The boys came home from school and undertook fact-finding missions to the site - our beach hut - returning with progress reports. Finally Miles ran in and vanished again with a complicit grin and a table lamp badly hidden under his jacket. This looked promising. Possibly a moment worth getting wet for. Outside I bent into the wind round the edge of the hen house then raised my eyes to the dark horizon. Rain beat against my face and drizzled down my neck, but down on the shore I could see a light.

Hurrah to the successful erection of our first wind turbine - named Leemill in honour of the helpful visitor. It generates 400 watts - five thousand times less than each of those huge 2 mega watt turbines that are being built at Spurness Windfarm on the south end of Sanday (unfortunately not for the direct energising of the island's community). But it's lighting our beach hut and keeping the batteries full of electrical energy that we have yet to make use of. A few more of these and we'll be cutting ourselves off from the national grid.

Market garden ~ *September*

On this rare, windless, sun-filled morning everything - birds and animals, barley fields and ocean - is still, at peace, calm and silent. Even the sound of the Landrover engine is intruding on the silence of the island. I should have cycled or walked - my journey is short - but a large box of veggies awaits me at my destination so I need the vehicle.

I turn off the road and park between a low wall and a greenhouse. With engine off I drink in the atmosphere of this orderly market garden. Over the wall is a neat, sheltered, lettuce bed. Beyond the greenhouse are regimented rows of well mulched leeks, parsnips, onions and along the east wall some thoroughly staked and wired peas. The whole garden is surrounded by wall or green-netted fencing. Shelter is paramount to the success of veggie growing up here.

A door opens over at the house. I turn to see Mag approaching. We discuss the weather, of course, and hope this is the start of a late summer. Then Mag and Davo take me through the low door of the byre to show me around the poultry side of their farm. Davo opens the door of an incubator to show me a few freshly hatched chicks. These gorgeous wee creamy-yellow chicks will shortly be taken over to the brooder to join their hatchling mates. In the incubator a few eggs remain, perhaps still to hatch.

We go out through the back of the byre and into one of a series of sheds. As we go in the smell of paraffin hits me and a disconcerting stack of long wooden boxes stored in the entrance reminds me that Davo is also the island's undertaker. I focus on the brooder instead. This is a low-lidded cage where the newborn chicks can grow in warmth and safety until they are two or three weeks old. To either side of the cage are feed troughs providing chick crumbs and water. The essential warmth comes from paraffin heaters underneath the cage - the original underfloor heating system perhaps.

Back out in the grassy yard hens, turkeys, ducks and two feral geese range freely. Most of the hens are the elegant black and white of the Light Sussex Cross, but Davo points out a funny wee black hen with a tufty head. A relative brought down some pale green eggs from Shetland, which, on incubation, produced these Shetland hens.

Further huts have their doors open to provide nesting and roosting homes for the free-rangers. At the end is another closed door. This houses the six week old chicks who are ready to be sorted. The girls, with their smaller pink combs, get to go into the stage four hut and continue to mature until they become point-of-lay hens at twenty weeks. The boys, condemned by their bright red combs, are labelled cockie-chickens and destined for the pot. Lastly there's a shed especially for the Light Sussex cockerel and three pure bred hens. All the eggs destined to become chicks come from here. All the eggs collected from the free range hens are for selling.

Beyond the sheds is a field of cabbages, turnips, broccoli, curly kale and cauliflowers and this brings me back to my mission - to collect my box of veggies for the week. It is already packed for me, heavy with tatties, leeks, cabbage, spring onion, lettuce, a neap and two trays of pea pods, all fresh from the garden. Eight years ago Mag and Davo sold their cattle and started a market garden. In the early years they grew a wider range - everything from beetroot to corn-on-the-cob, aubergine to spinach, cole rabi to courgette.

Most things grew well: despite our northern latitude we have a mild, maritime climate with few frosts. The limiting factor in this small, island population was what they could sell. So, after some interesting experiments the range was streamlined to include only those most marketable. And with all their other roles - ambulance driver, undertaker, NFU Insurance Agent and hen and arable farmers - the veggies grown have to involve the least work for the greatest return.

As I write I'm snapping fresh peas out of their pods and filling my mouth with their delicious juicy crispness. My desk is increasingly littered with the empty pods. I certainly hope the Rendalls keep growing these. (Must try to save some for the children.)

Bugbears ~ *September*

Nits, mites, mice, rabbits, nettles, ragwort and hogweed. These are some of the less delightful fellow inhabitants of our Orkney island. Nits. Well schools seem to breed them these days. Ever since the good old nit nurse was banished and the honour of dealing with nits was handed over to us parents, head lice have been having a field day. Yesterday the boys returned from school with news of fresh louse sightings. Nic and I set out our stall - nit comb, hair clippers, tea tree shampoo and conditioner - and took it in turns to attack the boys' unruly heads. This morning they are clipped, cleaned and conditioned and we can report "nul point" on the louse count.

Mites. Over the past weeks, since this year's hay was brought in, I have been noticing an unusual build up of pinkish dust on the byre floor. On closer inspection this "dust" appeared to be moving. Seven-year-old Fenning's magnifying insect inspector kit confirmed my suspicions that the dust was in fact millions of tiny insects. My skin crawled. Further inspection of the outbuildings revealed that these insects were not only on the floor but also all over the feed bins and saddlery which were in the tack room under the hay loft.

Storage mites, as I have now discovered from various books, are members of the Acarina order of Arachnids: the smallest of the spider family. These eight legged beasties proliferate in feedstuffs like hay and grain where they feed on fungal growth prompted by damp storage conditions. Although probably always present in smaller numbers, a wet summer and harvest time prompts their best turnout - which can exceed one thousand mites per gram of hay. The mind boggles. Known as "bakers' itch" elsewhere (and I don't even want to contemplate the insinuation in that nickname), up here in Orkney they are blamed for fairly high levels of asthma and hay fever among farmers. I haven't come across an Orcadian name for them yet, but there must be one (if not several).

Every conscientious mouse is seeking a cosy winter home right now and a large number of them seem to think our house would suit. Fenning is busy again with his traps. Having given up on the idea of keeping a mouse as a pet, he now takes his frequent victims out to the byre cats. But they only show mild, sidelong interest: they have plenty of their own to catch. That's when they are not bringing home rabbits for my approval.

Rabbits have a strange distribution here on Sanday. Super-abundant in some areas, they are entirely absent in others, for no apparent reason. They also come in a wider variety of colour than I have ever seen before, with a predominance of pretty blacks and greys. Until the cats brought me their first rabbit I hadn't seen any on our land and naively hoped (despite large diggings in the sandy soil of our top fields) that we were free of them. Perhaps our resident ravens have been keeping the numbers down.

Our fields, having not been cattle or sheep grazed for some years, are edged by a healthy array of wild plants. Or, depending on your viewpoint (whether you are a bird or a farmer), are horribly weedy. Nettles, thistles, ragwort and hogweed raise their white, purple and yellow flowers to the skies all along our boundaries. Ragwort, poisonous to horses, is mercifully minimal thanks to my horse loving predecessor and I have only had to dig out a few this summer. Hogweed, however, is rife and has caused my delightful new Clydesdale horse the indignity of a blistered nose - the unhappy consequence of eating hogweed while basking in the sun. How's a horse to know that? Next spring she will be coated in suncream and I will wage war on the hogweed.

And nettles? Well they abound around our outbuildings and I've been hacking them down whenever I have time. But now, courtesy of Radio Orkney, I learn that they could be the next big thing in agriculture. Historically used as fibre for cloth (Mary Queen of Scots' table linen was allegedly made from nettles) these plants are also much loved by birds and insects and as such may be the perfect crop for both farmer and wildlife. Especially here in Orkney, where we apparently grow our nettles in extra king-size.

Mailboat ~ *September*

Rain lashes at my kitchen windows. Wind moans through the annoying wee ventilators at the top of each. Last night a light bulb blew and fused all our lights. I haven't fixed the fuse yet. This morning I came through to a cold Rayburn. Out in the cold, wet day I tapped the oil tank and it rang hollow through and through. Empty. It can't be six months since we moved here and had the tank filled. April, May, June, July, August, September: eight-year-old Dale counts the months on his fingers then holds them up for me.

I phone our friendly, multi-tasking farmer, who delivers oil when he's not cutting barley or shifting cows or organising haulage or helping at the Spurness wind turbine construction site. I use his mobile phone - I assume he's never in one place for long enough to answer a land line. "Oh dear." He's not sure when the next oil tanker is due on the island, but he can bring me up a drum of oil before this evening so we can rev up the Rayburn in time for tea. Thank goodness for good neighbours.

Meanwhile the house is a bit dismal and the dogs need a walk. I don boots and jacket, hat and gloves (whatever happened to that Indian summer I kept predicting) and lazily opt to drive along the road to the turn-off I have in mind. I could easily have walked the whole way. I park on rough grass, well off the road, and we set off into the wind along a narrow ridge of land. The dogs rush ahead and tumble over a low wall into the surging sea. Then they're back, leaping up at me and shaking their salt-wet coats all over me. I skim stones into the sea to keep the dogs busy, away from me. I elect to walk along the slippery stones of the high shore rather than the rough grass of the inland side of the ridge. Up ahead I can see my destination: Black Rock jetty.

The jetty is a long slope of concrete running out and down into the sea. Along one side is a somewhat flimsy metal rail, along the other nothing but a vertical drop into the sea and a few metal rings set into the concrete, for tying up boats. A sign at the landward end dictates "Danger, Keep Off" but I walk a little way along so that I can look down through the clear waters to admire the swaying fronds of seaweed. At the seaward end of the jetty is another sign on a pole. It is facing away from shore, but I assume it warns passing boaters of the presence of this hulk of concrete. Stacked alongside the jetty are fishing creels and boxes and round in the shelter of Otterswick Bay there's a lone, moored, fishing boat. Someone uses this jetty, but it's not the hive of activity it once was.

Way back in the good old days (i.e. not so long ago) these north isles of Orkney only had a weekly steamer (ferry) service and for North Ronaldsay there was only a boat into Kirkwall once a fortnight. However there was a mail boat which ran between North Ronaldsay and Sanday three times a week and this served as a traveller's alternative for getting from that most remote of islands down to the big toon.

It wasn't an easy option. The mail boats were wee open boats, light enough to haul ashore on the smaller islands where there wasn't a pier. The Sanday - North Ronaldsay mail boat would land at Black Rock and, before the building of the jetty, it would be a case of scrambling across wet rocks or being lifted ashore by the boatman (latterly Big Johnny Tulloch). Then you had to get across Sanday - walking or hitching a ride - to her main port at Kettletoft to catch the steamer from there to Kirkwall. The Sanday boat also served Westray, Papay, Stronsay and Eday and could easily take eight hours to reach Kirkwall. Even in the best of weather, it was a long journey.

Beyond the jetty I walk on along a spit of land until its very end at Point of Nevin and look across to Colli Ness and all around the beautifully sheltered waters of Otterswick Bay. Six thousand years ago, so legend and recent research has it, this was willow woodland. But that's another story.

Back at the Landrover I find I've got mail. My replacement driving license from DVLA and a letter from America have been delivered onto my driver's seat. The island postal service no longer relies on very small boats but it still relies on posties with initiative.

Hurricanes ~ *October*

Living the idyll of remote island life, as I do up here in Orkney, I manage, for the most part, to veer away from the violence and tragedy of the world at large. I don't watch the news on TV at all, so my head isn't full of ghastly visuals. I listen to a national radio news summary about once a day, but I don't bombard my ears with hourly bulletins of fact, fiction and comment. I catch sight of a newspaper once a week but rarely make time to read it. This is not really anything to do with island life - it's perfectly possible to watch all the same TV images here as anywhere else in the UK - but much more of a personal decision. If I took in the average measure of media horror I would be a taut, twanging wire of stress and anxiety.

But every so often a phenomenon of nature attracts my sympathy. Bangladeshi floods, Japanese earthquakes, Australian bush fires, African drought. In recent weeks my attention has been drawn by the hurricanes doing their equinoctial rounds and revisiting their old haunts, wreaking havoc wherever they travel and leaving a trail of devastation and tragedy in their wake.

Hurricanes are winds of over 75mph, categorised on a scale of one to five: weak to devastating (anything over 155mph) with resultant damage correspondingly mild to catastrophic. Hurricanes alone may not do too much damage, but by their tempestuous behaviour they spawn the savage spin and lift of tornadoes and the deluge of the storm-surge - a dome of ocean water lifted and hurled ashore ahead of the storm, with fatal consequences for coasts and low altitude island communities.

So the chaos, mayhem and death toll in Haiti was Hurricane Jeanne stirring up trouble as she collided with the island of Hispaniola in the Caribbean stretch of the Atlantic hurricane belt. Once back over the open ocean she re-formed her tight eye and gathered strength, ready to pounce on Florida at 110mph. Jeanne is tenth on this year's list of Atlantic hurricanes, having been preceded by the likes of Bonnie, Charley, Frances and Ivan. Hurricanes are given alternately male and female names, working through the alphabet each year. There are six lists of names used in rotation i.e. the 2004 list was last used in 1998 and will appear again in 2010.

After the international news coverage of hurricane havoc across the Atlantic, we often see those same hurricane names (most recently Karl) appearing on our weather forecasts as "remnants of ex-hurricanes" giving us a final lash of their tails before their energies are entirely spent. But these Northern Isles also get whole hurricanes all to themselves. The most notable, still talked about in Orkney, were a series of three in the early 1950's.

In the early hours of a wintery night in January 1952 a 120mph (so only three on the one to five hurricane intensity scale) south-westerly blasted through Orkney, whipping off roofs, ripping out electricity and phone systems and demolishing any wooden buildings. The extensive Orkney hen industry was hardest hit, with huts collapsing or blowing away. The following day dead hens were strewn everywhere across the landscape. Collapsed or roofless cow byres left the poor beasts to weather the storm unprotected and ruined their winter feed stores. A Sanday man travelled through the air with his house - Wizard of Oz style - before coming to a mercifully safe landing.

A year later another storm hit, hurling 125mph winds at the whole of the east coast of Britain. Kirkwall had her sea defences breached and her sea-front roads flooded and torn up. And one of the North Isles ferries, Earl Thorfinn, famously set off from Kirkwall to Westray and ended up in Aberdeen, the heroic young captain having made the life-saving decision to turn her around, in the teeth of the hurricane, and let her run with the wind instead of against it. In November of 1953 a third hurricane hit Orkney, whipping away her recently cut grain harvest and leaving the cows hungry for another winter. Three hurricanes in less than three years must have caused a lot of climate change conversations.

Fifty years on Orkney's climate is always lively and she suffers stormy weather on a regular basis, but we haven't felt the wrath of an extreme hurricane for a while....

Woods ~ *October*

When, from the hilly comforts of Perthshire, I first mentioned this island of Sanday to my father he studied the map I proffered and, with wry humour, pronounced it a spit of sand unlikely to survive the next decent storm. Four years on and the island really feels quite large and solid and doesn't seem to be vanishing before our very eyes or sinking underfoot. In fact it's easy to forget that we live on a very small landmass. It is, after all, a whole twenty miles long.

Easy, that is, until a stranger from the distant realms of the University of Glasgow comes along and undertakes some pretty basic research to prove that our island is, shall we say, not the same shape as it used to be. It is, you guessed it, getting smaller. Said scientist, one Alistair Rennie (who now works for Scottish Natural Heritage), came to our school a few weeks ago and succinctly described his research to a packed classroom. The title of his talk - "The Bonnie Woods of Otterswick" - was lure enough, for Sanday has no woodland, barely a single tree, and Otterswick is a bay of sparkling sea, renowned for its cockle harvest at low tide. Some mistake surely.

So Nic, me and the boys went along to the evening's entertainment at the appointed hour and were amazed at what we heard, saw and touched. Based on 19th century surveys, which showed a submarine forest along the west coast of Otterswick, and a variety of folklore and poetry mentioning the "Bonnie woods..." Alistair had decided to take a look at the site.

With the help of a mechanical digger (and that very busy farmer I mentioned recently) holes were dug along the beach until, at hole six, they struck gold. Well not gold of course but tree stumps, about one metre below the present sandy surface. Subsequent radio carbon analysis suggested that these trees were alive and kicking 6500 years ago and close examination of their structure suggested that they were the remnants of willow trees. As a finale he produced some bits of the actual wood out of a poly bag and allowed us each to gingerly touch and prod this ancient matter. Awesome.

One of his slides showed an old map of Sanday on which he pointed out areas of land where we now have sea inlets and large Nesses (peninsulas of farmable land) where we now have rocky skerries. One of these caused a stir from the audience - there were folk present who could remember a proper road to Start Point, which is now a tidal island. Interestingly enough, on the other side of the island there are a set of beaches that grew and infilled a bay, at the same time as Otterswick was being inundated. It is, according to SNH's Coastal Geomorphologist, "all to do with the key role of sediment supply on the behaviour of the shoreline". You win some you lose some.

Armed with this new insight into our environment Nic and I took a walk (after a sweaty morning of stacking our freshly harvested straw bales into the byre) along the west side of Otterswick. I noticed after a while that we were both looking at our feet rather than our usual habit of staring vacantly out to sea. Then I spotted a knarled length of dense black material and pounced on it. Could it be ancient forest remains? We tore at it with all the scientific finesse of three year olds discovering doughnuts and came to the disappointing conclusion that it was nothing more exciting than petrified tyre rubber, circa. 1977.

Fascinating in its own right, one useful aspect of this research is that it builds up a picture of sea level rise over the centuries and helps to narrow down a prediction for the future. And the answer? Well, based on this particular model, our seas could rise by anything from about one to seventy centimetres by the year 2080. That's one helluva margin of error and, given that our house is only five metres above sea level and our land runs right down to the beach, quite pertinent. Maybe we don't have to worry too much, but we must remember to tell the grandchildren. They might not be inheriting as much land as they expect.

Collectives ~ *October*

I have always had a wee thing about collective nouns - a parliament of herons, a cacophony of corvids, a parade of penguins - and so on. If I'm stuck for one I make it up - a chaos of children, a madness of midges, a hunger of seagulls. I mentioned this to my learned uncle ages ago and yesterday he emailed me a list of some lesser known ones thrown up by a competition run through his village magazine.

Some are obvious when you think about it: a crash of rhinoceri, a leap of leopards, a mob of kangaroos. Some are more obscure: a gam of whales (not pod?), a grist of bees (not hive?), a husk of hares, a muster of peacocks (I've seen peacocks strut and flounce their feathers and flurry up and down from trees or rooftops, but I wouldn't say that they mustered). Some are just gorgeous: a sleuth of bears, a watch of nightingales, a kindle of kittens.

For us this week's collective nouns are flock, shire and rot. (OK, so I made the last two up.) We have, at last, a flock of fifty sheep arriving soon. In its recent history our fifty acre farm has been used for either cattle or crops. The fences, where they exist at all, are three or four strands of barb wire - not enough to keep a woolly sheep at bay. In the barley fields the fences have been entirely removed. So we have many metres of shire wire to put up if we are to keep our new sheep at home.

And then there is rot. Our old stone outbuildings are looking remarkably healthy for their age. Their walls are upright, straight and true (except in one place where a tractor unfortunately set off in the wrong direction). Their slated roofs are only slightly saggy and only leak a wee bit in a couple of places. But their wooden doors are sadly rotting, flaking and disintegrating, their hinges and latches rusted through. What with the salt-laden wind and the lashing rain of an Orkney climate, buildings here need constant maintenance to stop their steady and inevitable slide back to nature.

Today we set to. Whenever I see Nic he is measuring or sawing or swearing at an ancient screw head that has rusted into place and won't budge. Whenever he sees me I'm striding along fence lines and scowling when I lose count of my paces. Or I'm swinging imaginary gates, working out where they should go and which way they should be hinged. We meet at the kitchen table for a plate of leek and tattie soup, our backs warmed by the Rayburn, and flick through our newly arrived post.

A thick manila envelope at the bottom of the pile turns out to be the most interesting. We've been accepted on to the Rural Stewardship Scheme (RSS). Out come maps and lists of all the things we have agreed to do - hedging, fencing, mowing and grazing regimes, extensive and unharvested cropping. We struggle to remember the myriad rules and regulations - it is, after all, six months since we submitted our application.

In addition to our new field fencing there are fences to be put up along the water margins of our wetland and around our arable fields. It all adds up to about 3000 metres of fence line. According to the blurb this is to be completed in the first quarter of our five year agreement. We search for a start date for the first quarter and find 1st September 2004. Help! We're already half way through it. If we really have to get all the fencing done by the end of November we had better get out there. Or, on second thoughts, we had better phone a man we know with a fencing machine.

Meanwhile, on the family calendar, two people have birthdays to celebrate tomorrow. My aforementioned uncle will, I think, be blowing out more than eighty candles on his cake. And our middle son, Dale, will be nine and we've rashly allowed him to invite his friends over to party the afternoon away. Would that be a nightmare of nine-year-olds?

Geese ~ *October*

Never imagine that your past won't catch up with you. It might take a while - by definition it kind of has to take a while. But it always gets to you in the end: usually just when you have forgotten all about it.

And so it was for me and geese. Several lifetimes ago, fresh out of Stirling University with a biology degree, I moved to the Hebridean island of Islay to do things with wild arctic geese. I identified them (in birders' slang: barnacles, white-fronts, greylags, pink-feet, brents, canadas), counted them, caught them, weighed them, ringed them (or, rather, held them while someone bolder than me clamped the metal rings onto their legs) studied their feeding habitats (scrutinised a whole lot of grass) and came to some rather less than Earth-shattering conclusions (barnacle geese, for instance, prefer to munch on a short, fertile sward of rye grass and clover) that pretty much any observant farmer could have told me in the first place.

But most of all I counted. I counted geese on my study plots for my own research and I counted geese across the whole island for RSPB (The Royal Society for the Protection of Birds) and for SNH (Scottish Natural Heritage). Sometimes I even counted geese on other islands like Tiree and Coll. I know there are people who have counted more geese than me, but I've counted quite a lot. Enough. Or so I thought.

When I moved to Orkney I rejoiced at being able to enjoy seeing birds all around the island, doing their thing, without having to document them. Geese were tricky in this respect: quite often I would stop myself mid-count and remember that I no longer had to. I could actually just enjoy watching them fly over without needing to know how many there were or even what type of geese they were.

Now, five years later, when my binoculars have been relegated to the kitchen windowsill for nothing more nerdy than checking on the sheep and horses, someone goes and asks me to count how many arctic geese have arrived on Sanday for the winter. Sacre bleu! What's to be done? Well of course old habits die hard and I can't resist. Before I can stop myself I'm eagerly studying the map with the regular count volunteer who has asked me to step in while she's away.

On the appointed date the boys and I set off early through the grey world of an overcast October sky and head for Loth - the most southerly point of this wee island. Spurness - an erstwhile favourite haunt for the geese - has been somewhat disturbed by the erection of three massive wind turbines. We make the most of this goose counting excuse to drive along the newly forged tracks directly under the turbines. There aren't any geese here, of course, but being so close to the turbines is tremendous.

Just up the road I spot a flock of geese on a barley stubble field and then I remember - greylag geese love freshly harvested barley fields when they first arrive onto their wintering grounds. After this first count of 454 geese I'm back in my stride. Nic drives admirably, suffering my "stop!" and "quick up to the next brow!" commands, and finds out why "birders" are such dangerous drivers. In the back of the Landrover the boys plug into a whodunit story tape and peer out from steamed up windows, occasionally shouting "geese, mum!". At Kettletoft we stop for a picnic on the pier while I scan the distant fields of Elsness across the bay. By midday we have covered most of the island. We now have two complications: our next location is across a tidal sand-flat and the tide is still too high, and Nic and I are due to Lifeguard the swimming pool for the afternoon session. Excellent. Two hours later the boys are happily exhausted, we've done our bit for the community and the tide has dropped.

Out beyond the sand flats at Cata is a surprising acreage of fertile farmland. Nic engages diff-lock to negotiate the still wet sands (we've sunk here before) and we whiz across to Tresness. Through a gate and along a mud-rutted track we find our quarry. Several hundred geese lift off a muddy field and hesitate obligingly while I count them before they drop down once more into the obscurity of the folds and contours of land. It's a fitting end to a great day out.

Fencing ~ *October*

For the most part the pace of island life is probably slower than your average city existence. But it ain't necessarily so. Sometimes one is caught out by a rare combination of efficiency and workaholism.

Urged on by our Rural Stewardship Scheme (RSS) requirement for some 3000metres of new stock fencing, Nic phoned the best and fastest fencer we have come across in our short history as farm owners, to see if he could help us out. This man lives on Orkney Mainland - a lengthy ferry ride away from us - and we hoped to persuade him and his fencing machinery to come out to our island for what could be a good week's work. We were thinking late November, whenever he could fit us in, before Christmas would be great.

"I'm here in Sanday" I could hear Tommy's booming voice even though it wasn't me holding the phone, "come and see me tonight, after dark, and bring your farm map". We're not very good at going out at night - it's been so long - but spurred on by this promising news we loaded up the boys and set off into the rain squalls of the night. Along a sand track we reached the holiday cottage and there he stood, larger than life, deep-voiced, dogmatic, eyes full of mirth and twinkle set in his swarthy, weathered face.

We showed him our map and he told us all the options: square stabs, round stabs, electric wire, barb wire, half-shire, full shire, concrete strainers, wooden strainers, gates in anything from light to heavy, 10 foot to 15 foot. We argued the toss a bit, made decisions and agreed to order up the materials for delivery ASAP - the first 700 metres could be fenced for us within the next few days.

Meantime our task was to take out all the old fencing. Meantime meantime we were actually trying to get away for a few days, to introduce the boys to the concept of hills and trees with a walking holiday on Hoy. Well, we reasoned, old fencing can't take that long to houwk out; we'll manage that when we get back.

Four days later and our fencing materials have arrived in Sanday. As we drive home Tommy waves from a roadside fence he's just finishing. Right, we'd better get on. We hitch a borrowed trailer (must buy one) to our Landrover and set off across our nearest field to rip out its fence. The stabs are rotten twigs leaning at sickly angles. The barb wire hangs in rusty, sagging, loops. Yet they are curiously reluctant to be parted from each other. With wire cutters and thick gloves we work in tandem, cutting and winding up the spiky wire, pulling and pushing and kicking out the slippery, splintery posts. Rain insidiously seeps through our overalls. As dusk encroaches we have a full trailer and a terrible thirst on us - beer and a warm kitchen beckon. But for all our labour we have only cleared 300 metres of fenceline. Slow progress, room for improvement.

Next morning we're in various states of undress at the kitchen table (it is still the holidays after all) when our plumber and electrician arrives to measure up. We're changing the utility room to a bathroom, the bathroom to a bedroom. It all makes good sense really. Next, two tractors arrive, one with a mechanical hammer on the front, the other with a trailer-load of fencing materials on the back. Eek! The fencers have arrived and the race is on to rip out the old before they whang in the new.

Then a car arrives. It's Ian, who has been fencing all the twiddly bits around our house and garden that a tractor can't reach. He's only too happy to help with the greater task of fencing the fields. Our normally quiet wee farm is suddenly a hive of activity. The horses and sheep keep watch from a respectful distance but make no attempt to cross their temporarily fenceless boundaries. And Tommy, the big man himself, is a man on a mission. He moves at speed up and down the lines, hammering stabs (his helper fearlessly holding them vertical), feeding out lines of top wire, unrolling shire wire. Strainer holes are dug out, the impossibly heavy concrete strainers dropped in and rocks thumped in all around each. A fenceline that we thought was OK is whipped out and replaced before we can demure. He's a hard man to keep up with, is Tommy, but as day dips into night the last gate fills the last gap and the beer cans are cracked. Job done.

Lady Helen ~ *November*

In the inky darkness before dawn I am already up and out in the feed shed, moving quietly by the light of my head torch. I fill two buckets with molassen chaff, cool mix, sugar beet, plus a dash of oil, garlic granules and farriers' friend. As soon as I pour hot water over the feed a heady aroma fills the air and I can hear the horses stirring and snickering in their boxes. They aren't used to being fed so early, but they are certainly not complaining.

I take them their breakfast and watch them tuck in. But Chuck (my niece's American Quarter horse), wise guy that he is, is suspicious. He knows something's up and looks enquiringly over his door at me rather than nosing in to his feed. He's absolutely right. What I want to do is close the top half of his door so that I can lead Lady Helen - my gorgeous big Clydesdale mare - away without upsetting either of them. They are, after all, in lurve. Separation anxiety antics are likely to manifest themselves. Eventually Chuck puts head to bucket and I whip the top door shut then quietly open Helen's door. She pricks her ears and obligingly tiptoes out of the yard with me. We set off along the track together as the first streaks of golden light are pouring across the green fields and blue sea all around us. What a breathtakingly beautiful morning.

Lady helen and I walk for half a mile or so to get to our borrowed horse lorry. It seemed sensible not to risk driving it along our potholed and tightly cornered track. She's a great horse to walk beside, her long swinging stride sets a fast pace and she observes the world with fascination. But she keeps her dinner-plate sized feet carefully clear of mine and she walks shoulder to shoulder by my side without my having to pull back or push on. She's an extremely well behaved horse.

At the horse lorry she walks straight up the ramp and shuffles round to her sideways position where Nic ties and partitions her in. Even in this full size lorry a Clydesdale has to stand at an angle and take up the space allocated for two "normal" horses. I stay and chat to Helen and from the lorry window we watch Nic jog back home through the gossamer morning light. He has to let Chuck out into his field for the day and collect up the boys, who we have left with strict instructions to dress, eat, pee and get their schoolbags ready. A tall order for these three sleepyheads, but they rise to the occasion admirably.

All aboard the lorry, we set off around our narrow bay road. In the centre of the island we drop off the boys at school. It's only 8.15am but they can play footie in the playground. Then Nic and I rumble on down to the ferry terminal with our precious load. We have quite a wait in the ferry queue (in my apprehension we set off far too early) and the lorry shifts from side to side as Helen begins to get restless. I've come prepared for this. I wriggle through the lorry cab to the kitchen/living area and thence through a door to the horse quarters. Helen snorts at my offering - a soap-on-a-rope style of horse lick - which I tie up within her reach. I've brought two, aniseed flavour for this morning's journey and banana flavour for our return tonight. They work a treat.

Our one and a half hour ferry trip is mercifully calm and uneventful. Then we're on the road and trucking across Orkney Mainland to our destination - a stable yard near Stenness and two professional horsey folk who are waiting to meet us, or rather, to meet our horse. Nic lowers the ramp and I lead Lady Helen down into a wealth of new experiences. Her nostrils flare and her big brown eyes widen in amazement. On one side are four horses in a field, all trotting over to take a look at this new arrival. Round to the right is a sand schooling yard but Helen swings her hind quarters and turns on a sixpence to look left at a block of stables where yet more horses are whinnying their greetings to her.

It's a big day out for a young girl who has barely left home before, but Helen is a good sport and behaves impeccably throughout the day. And the reason for our trip? Well all you mainlanders will laugh, but all this effort, all these hours on the boat, are just to get to an appointment with a saddle fitter. But such is island life. Things aren't just so easy to achieve, facilities aren't so easy to reach, experts aren't so readily available. Next month we have to do the whole trip again for a dental appointment. That's a horse dentist, not a human one. I'd never go to this much trouble for myself.

Post ~ *November*

Christmas is a' coming and the goose is getting fat. I'm reminded of this lyric as Nic and I walk over our back hill this morning, to post a batch of parcels at our local post office. Our nearest post office is only a couple of miles over our back hill, on our adjoining farm. It's a good chance for us to stretch our legs, breathe the clear air, check the sheep and horses and take a proud look over our new fencing. And it is also an opportunity for a chat: although we both work from home, we sit at our respective computers in different rooms. Sometimes we even email each other - how daft is that?

Our version of working from home could be seen as a tad quirky. In between bouts at the computers we flit off to feed animals, move sheep, fix a fence or dig up the yard to find the plumbing routes (this is my most recent venture and I can boast success). When I am writing I'm usually staring out of the window and I have to admit that I'm not very good at answering the phone.

The ringing sound often gets mixed in with whatever I am dwaming about and it takes persistence for it to reach my conscious level. So before I get to it, the phone might be answered by a passing boy-child or the plumber who is fixing up our new bathroom. It might get answered by the answering machine. Or it may even get diverted to a mobile phone in Nic's pocket, where it may or may not get heard above the high winds and the whang of the hammer as Nic staples our new stock fence. All this is OK because even our seven year old is more organised about taking down details than I am.

Whenever we have mail to post we congregate before noon - the post office is open until 12.30 - and tog up for a walk in Orkney's wildest weather, post and parcels in a rucksack. Round the back of our big byre is a very muddy track. To our left we overlook our barley stubble field. Greylag geese lift off at our arrival, but drop down again only a few yards further away. The spilt barley is too good to fly away from. Beyond is our wetland, temporarily hugely enlarged by a rainy season worthy of the tropics. The local birdlife love it and have moved in en masse: it is hooching with ducks, gulls and waders. Beyond the wetland is our wee beach, complete with hauled out seals, and the sea. To our right is the grassy paddock that backs onto our yard. The horses trot over to us then plod along the fenceline with us until we leave them at the corner gate.

Over the hill is a whole new vista. On a clear day we can see the whole of the north end of Sanday from here, plus North Ronaldsay just across the ocean. Below us are two farms. We follow the track round to the one on our right and Nic hangs back with the dogs while I go in through the farmhouse door. The post office is actually the front porch of the house, a short counter half-occluding the way through to the main house.

I call "hello" to Irene and breathe in the heavenly aroma of whatever she's cooking up for dinner. Trying to keep my muddy boots on the doormat I hand over the parcels and we both squint at the scales. While her new-fangled computer churns out labels and receipts we chat about the weather and what's on around the island. We never gossip, of course. Occasionally someone else arrives to post something and sometimes the postie turns up to empty the post box. Then we can exchange parcels, thus saving him a trip up our track.

Then I'm back out into the weather, whatever it is. Probably because of Irene's cooking, we always seem to talk about food all the way home. Today is no exception. As we round the bend onto our track we are approached by another neighbouring farmer. He's raising turkeys for Christmas and do we want one. I hesitate: we know several folk who raise turkeys and we don't want to do any of them out of business. So we say yes, please and I mentally pencil in turkey for New Year as well. And maybe another one for Miles' birthday.

Time and tide

~ Winter
2004

Hoy ~ *November*

Two years ago I escaped domesticity and ran off with my best buddy for a romantic weekend among the heathery hills of Hoy. A month ago eldest son Miles finally voiced what had obviously been a small irk in his mind ever since that weekend. Why hadn't we taken the boys with us to Hoy - they wanted to see it too.

To avoid waffley explanations about the need for occasional romantic escape - even from the most gorgeous of children - I simply countered with, "OK, let's go there for the school holidays". It was hardly the sun, sea and sand vacation I had had in mind, but que sera sera: a dose of worthy striding in waterproofs and stout boots would probably do us more good.

On the appointed morning we load up children, dogs, warm clothes and a stack of books and games and head for our North Isles ferry. Over on Orkney Mainland Nic (that best buddy, now best hubby) and twelve-year-old Miles raid Dounby Stores (Orkney's best version of a mini-supermarket) with their much discussed menu list. They tell me I'm on holiday, so not allowed to shop. This turns out to be a neat way of filling the trolley with tinned beans, soup, spaghetti, tuna fish and (shock horror) corned beef, a pile of "just re-heat" pastry items and an unseemly amount of chocolate. Hmm. Judging by the menu this is to be a boys' own camping trip.

We board our second boat of the day at the southern port of Houton and shiver on another rain-lashed deck while we churn across a choppy Scapa Flow. I'm cold to my bones and can't quite recall why we are doing this. Reaching Hoy in the late afternoon we drive straight up the island's east side then take a left to negotiate the even narrower road across to Rackwick Bay. And there is our holiday cottage nestling in the bay, dwarfed by the massive cliffs of Craig Gate beyond. The boys are astonished: Hoy is so completely different from Sanday. Where we have flat land and beaches, Hoy has rugged hills and craggy cliffs. Where we have the green and gold of grass and sand, Hoy has the black of peat and rock, the brown and purple of heather.

We have three missions: to scale the dizzy heights of Ward Hill (only 479m, but because you set off from sea level it's quite a climb), to walk around the cliff tops to the Old Man of Hoy - Orkney's famous 450ft sea stack - and to visit the trees of Berriedale wood, one of Britain's most northerly native woodlands.

Our first morning dawns dry-ish and sunny-ish with smatterings of rain on the sharp wind. Not brilliant, but not bad. Getting five people waterproofed and booted up in a very small porch is a laugh, but at length we are all outside, dogs on leads, picnics in rucksacks, breakfast pastries settling nicely in our bellies. The boys take on the challenge of Ward Hill with all the high spirits and energy of mountain hares. They leap and bounce over the heather, giggle when they fall in the peat bog and race each other to the next rocky outcrop. At the steeper ground seven-year-old Fenning huffs and puffs a bit but the first bar of chocolate lures him up to the summit of this lion of a hill.

Day two is my most worrisome. The cliff-top walk around the steep contours of Moor Fea to the Old Man of Hoy is not really so dangerous, but add three bouncy children and two hare-crazed dogs who have never known anything but the safety of flat land and you have a slightly nerve-wracking situation to control. Then Fenning decides this is his day to be a leader and he sets of like a professional cross-country runner. In my efforts to keep him in sight we pretty much run all the way. "Tuaks of the Boy" is a perilous ledge of land from where you can look over at the Old Man. I make everyone get down on their bellies and crawl. The views are stupendous, but this is not my favourite location.

By far everyone's favourite walk is through Berriedale woods. The birch, rowan, willow and aspen trees huddling into a deep cleft in the hillside are very beautiful and the ice-cold, sparkling water running down through the gorge is a delight. But then the boys dub it the jungle walk, which leads me to believe that they haven't seen enough big trees in their lives. Perhaps it's time to take them around the world again.

Stock judging ~ *December*

Four years of this Orkney island life and I have only just found out about the annual stock judging competition, hosted by a different farm in Sanday each autumn. This year it is to be held at Lopness Farm, at the north end of the island. We find out about it by chance: nine-year-old Dale has arranged to link up with a friend there and we, of course, are his taxi service.

On a still, cold, grey day we drive along to the tail of this dragon shaped island. Taking the narrow lighthouse road, we then turn off down a farm track to the house and byres ahead. Beyond the buildings is a sharp, rocky drop to the foreshore and then the huge sweep of the Bay of Lopness, ice-grey waters shifting restlessly along her anaemic sands.

A jumble of cars, landrovers and tractors are parked outside a long, slatted byre. We manoeuvre into a gap and join the throng of folk within. A few surprised faces greet us - this looks to be a gathering strictly for the farming folk - but we are given a warm welcome and a couple of jovial comments about our ability to judge beasts (that's the head, there's the tail, they should have four legs each). Then we are each given a square of green card and a pencil. The rules of play are explained: each enclosure contains four beasts, each with a letter, A,B,X or Y, spray-painted onto its bum. We have to judge them, best to worst, and write down the letters on our card accordingly. There are eight pens, each holding four of: cows, heifers, stots (steers), calves, ewes, gimmers, store lambs and fat lambs.

We start with the cows. We are apparently looking for a sharp shoulder line, good broad muscle, a long back, deep chest and strong-boned legs. Well, they all look large and black. Try as we might, we can't see much to distinguish them from each other. An artist friend is having a go too and says she's going for the one with the prettiest face. I'm thinking they must need good child-bearing hips, whatever that looks like on a cow. Nic is studying their legs. Things don't get any easier with the heifers and stots (the girl and boy youths of the cow world) and I get into a rhythm of choosing my favourite, then my least favourite, then writing the two remaining letters randomly into the middle slots. It's a lottery.

We take a breather before moving on round to the sheep pens. A weak winter sun is slanting through the slatted walls of the byre, casting stripes of dust-moted light across animals and people alike. The sweet, acrid smell of silage feed fills the air like fermenting mead beer. In a regiment of boiler suits - red, green and blue - the island's farmers ponder the beasts with deep concentration. Kids in red wellies scoot in and out of adult legs, making their own judgements. An old sheepdog lies belly-flat, eyes in sharp focus, resolutely guarding the sheep pens.

Right then, on with the sheep judging. As the proud new owners of fifty-six ewes we reckon we should have a better eye for a sheep than a cow. The first pen sports four Texel ewes - we can tell that much, but again we are stumped when it comes to the finer points of sheep conformation. This time we're looking for breadth of head, shoulder and back and filled loins and gigots. If we could just shave off all that wool we might be able to see the subtle differences. The category I feel clearest on is in the last pen: fat lambs should surely be just that, so I list them in order, fattest to thinnest.

With all the green cards collected in, two oil barrels and an old door are employed as a table for the judges to tot up the scores and work out the winners. A complex point system is used to allow for how close to the professional judge's decision each entrant gets. If you put the best cow fourth you'll get fewer points than if you put her second, and so on. Meanwhile there is soup or tea, or maybe something stronger, in the farmhouse kitchen for anyone who wants a warm through.

At length, the results are announced. Nic and I get middling scores and both do better on the cows than the sheep. To her astonishment our artist friend wins the ladies' trophy. She claims beginner's luck but I'd say it's her critical eye and the fact that, obviously, pretty cows and sheep have more fun.

Dracula ~ *December*

The lights are down, the moon is up. Werewolves are howling from the depths of the gloomy forest. At the Castle of the Black Lake, the blood-thirsty Count is plotting to capture his next innocent victim. It's Friday night at the Sanday Community Hall and we have been transported by a drink-crazed airline pilot to the ghoulish realms of Transylvania.

Every so often the energetic and dedicated staff of our wee island school decide to put on a theatre production. This year it is, as you may have guessed, Dracula Spectacula. With one third of the island's school pupils on stage and as many kids and adults backstage, this is a big show for a small community. Auditions took place and rehearsals began way back before the summer holidays. School staff, parents and many other folk have been roped in to lend their expertise to every aspect of the production. Costumes, make-up, art, scenery, props, special effects, lighting, technical assistant, choreographer, musicians, sound engineer, and projectionist: the backstage crew list is impressively professional.

The audience have been invited to earn themselves a strip of free raffle tickets by coming along in fancy dress. With that in mind, Nic and I dropped in on Kirkwall's fine joke shop last week and came out with an armful of wigs, make-up, glue-on fangs, talons, vampire blood and the like. I love the chance to dress up and it doesn't happen often on this remote and windswept isle. So, dolled up to the nines as, respectively, a devil, a ghost and a couple of old vampires, Dale, Fenning, Nic and I drive to the show. (Miles is already there, being kitted out as a zombie.) En route we notice that the moon is full. Did our cunning theatre director pick the date of this first night so cleverly? Or are there dark forces at work already?

School is a buzz of activity and excitement. Classrooms one and two are designated boy and girl dressing and make-up rooms. The audience filters through a dimly lit corridor to the main hall, greeted by teachers and pupils in vampire attire. I notice sheep's wool features highly as a wig material. We are in farming country after all. In the orchestral pit, stage left, are three ghoulish fiddlers, resplendent in black-hair and tails. Stage right, an ancient, bulb-nosed, white-haired old wizard leans over his guitar.

The curtain goes up to a darkened stage, rapidly filling up with wafts of dry ice. A backdrop of projected images of skulls, skeletons, blood and gore set the scene for the spectacular, creeping entrance of the zombies and brides: the pitiful remnants of Dracula's possessed victims. Through spooky music a voice startles us from behind: Sister O'Stake strides forth, religious cross held aloft, banishing evil with her commanding voice. And so the first night of the show is underway, with no sign of first night nerves on any of the children's' faces.

One lovely aspect of small island life is that all these children are familiar to us and we can watch with fascination as they transform into character. In the face of such a challenge they seem suddenly older, more mature. From Dracula to the drunken pilot, Gretel to Genghis to the Glublick Addicts, Nadia Naive to Nick Necrophiliac they play their parts with courage, gusto and more than a little humour. As with all extra-curricular activities here (sport, music, publishing, chess to name but a few), the school role is small enough that everyone can have a go and flourish at something and consequently some rare talent is discovered.

The audience are the local community turned out in force. Tonight is a full house of 160 folk and tomorrow promises the same. Adding audience and participants you have some two-thirds of Sanday's population involved - a great accolade for the spirit of support in this close-knit community. Funds raised go toward the school trips fund and everyone has a good night out into the bargain.

In fact it's been so good that I think we'll try to squeeze into the hall again tomorrow night. Whatever shall I wear?

Rams ~ *December*

"You just get the Jacob sheep in, while I feed the horses, then we can both round up the big flock". Those were my fateful words, now ringing in Nic's ears as he completes his fifth lap of our six acre back field, the Jacob sheep obligingly running ahead, but baulking at the notion of actually trotting through the gate into the yard. The dogs, usually pretty good at rounding up sheep, seem distracted by the fact that I'm off feeding other animals. They usually get to fuss around me while I fill and distribute buckets.

Twenty minutes later I have fed the horses, the hens and the cat. I've put out a tempting trough of sheep nuts in the yard. I have noisily shaken a bucket. But our wee flock have forgotten that I used to feed them in here. They have reverted to their wild instincts. They're not up for this deal any more.

We are trying to get our Jacob ewes through to a wee pen at the back of the byres, thus freeing up the back field and the yard to bring in and sort our new flock of 56 ewes. When they arrived a few weeks ago we unloaded them into our grassiest field and left them, with a high energy sheep lick and a trough of nuts, to settle in. Now it's time to get them in for a proper look. I head out to help Nic and in a sudden flash of inspiration realise that the yard gate needs to be swung out the other way. With it jutting into the field it acts as a barrier to the sheep's endless circuit and diverts them neatly into the yard. Success at last.

First thing this morning we allocated a couple of hours to this whole sheep sorting job. Now we see an endless task ahead and begin to wonder if we'll get done before nightfall. But we are learning that farming tasks are contrary beasts: try to rush them, or even just put a time limit on them, and numerous complications and set-backs will conspire to mess up your plans. Give them all the time in the world and you'll be indoors with your feet up on the stove before you know it.

Bringing in the new flock involves moving them through one of our as yet unfenced fields - if we lose control of them at that point, then they could be off up the track with the whole island of Sanday at their disposal. We adopt that measured, unflustered attitude of those born and bred sheep farmers that we know. Nic opens gates and nonchalantly blocks off alternative routes, one dog at his heels. I saunter along behind our flock, my dog ranging to and fro just in front of me, and shut gates behind us. Eureka. Less than ten minutes later we have a yard full of sheep.

After all my ruminations on what breed of sheep we should keep, our new ewes are an eclectic mix of Cheviot, Shetland, Texel and Suffolk. You could call them a good starter flock. We'll be able to get to know the character, the pros and cons, of each breed. But there's still something missing. There's no show without punch. We need a ram.

Penned up in our sheep byre, and getting frisky, are two rams, delivered yesterday by one of the best sheep farmers on the island. One we have bought: a Texel ram lamb yet to prove his capabilities. The other we have borrowed: a majestically full grown Suffolk. Our task is to divide the flock into twenty or so ewes for the youngster and the rest for Mr. Mature. Then we have to fit our newly bought harnesses onto the rams and attach a colour block to the chest of each: blue for the Texel, green for the Suffolk. The colour rubs off on any mounted ewe, thus letting us know who's likely to be pregnant. Lastly we have to unite each ram with each sub flock of ewes and turn them out into different fields.

Keeping our "all-the-time-in-the-world" heads on we plod through each task, pausing at regular intervals to lean on a gate and discuss the next move. By midday the sheep are back out to grass and we're in the kitchen enjoying a plate of hot soup. Zen and the art of sheep farming: a philosophy for life?

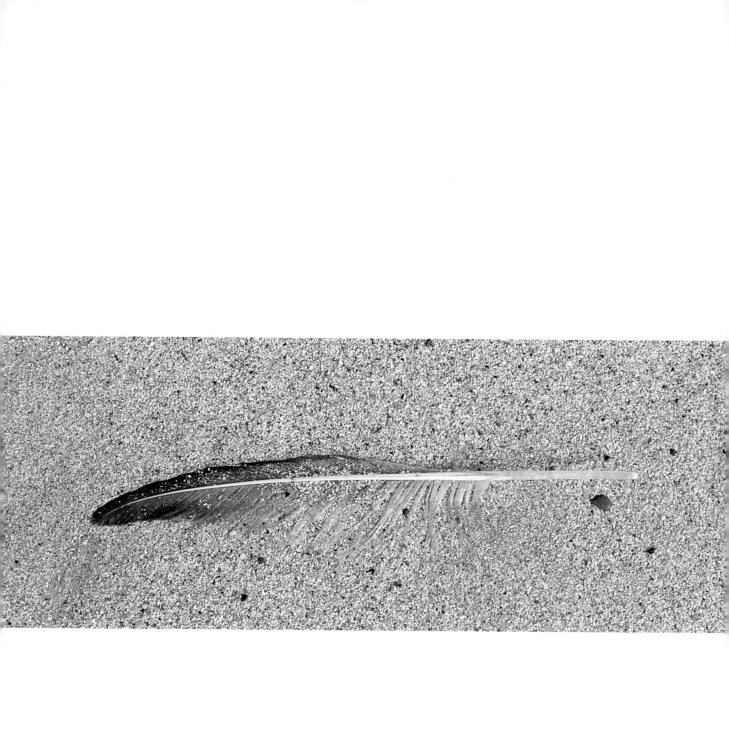

Table ~ *December*

I decided on my Christmas present for Nic a few months ago and began to organise it in early November. It threatened to be a tricky task. Among Nic's possessions, which emerged from Yorkshire in a removal lorry last May, was a gorgeous big old kitchen table. She was made of thick dark oak (or so we thought) and sported a (broken) wind out mechanism for a (missing) extra leaf. The whole piece was pretty shoogely and has got steadily worse, thanks to the leaping and climbing antics of three boys. At some point in the autumn I noticed the rakish angle of her gracefully turned legs, giving her a drunken aspect. Unless we did something soon, this table was surely going to collapse.

After an exhaustive search of the Yorkshire family barns and garages for the missing leaf, we gave up and were on the point of a Heath Robinson make-do-and-mend (hammer it together with six inch nails) job when I thought better of it. I had discovered a furniture maker on our neighbouring island of Eday - perhaps he could mend our table with a bit more finesse than ourselves.

So I phoned him up and described our table. We emailed him photos and he queried the two-tone colour of the surface. Oops, probably just ingrained dirt, I thought. Colin, the carpenter, said he could mend the table and make a new leaf. He named his very reasonable rate but I realised that this was going to be a more expensive venture than I'd imagined. It might have to be our joint Christmas present. The table was lovely and deserved proper care and attention after all her years of serving humans many and various. It's so easy to justify the spending of money when you put your mind to it.

We share a ferry with Eday and twice a week the route goes directly Sanday to Eday, a journey of about fifteen minutes. What could be simpler than to pop a table on the boat at Sanday and have it lifted off in Eday? Quite a lot apparently. The day we sent our table on her short journey the ferry's vehicle deck was so full that she could not be squeezed off at Eday. So she took a trip to Kirkwall, where she stayed in a warehouse for two nights before the Stronsay/Eday haulier took pity on her.

Colin received our table with enthusiasm. The base was of solid Russian Riga oak. The top was a mystery, the original oak having been replaced. It was hard to tell through all the layers of polish and dirt, but it could be American black walnut. The next phone call was disappointing: having stripped away the gunge, he could see that the top was made of Basf, another American wood which became popular in the early 20th century as it could be stained to closely resemble walnut.

I decided to find out more about our table and I learned that it was given as a wedding present to Nic's great grand parents in Halifax in 1870. No one can remember the top being replaced - perhaps it was already an old table when they were given it. I'm fascinated by old wood. An oak tree from Russia and a Basf tree from America, felled and sawn over a century ago, yet now serving as the hub of family life on a treeless island in Orkney. We chose walnut for the new central leaf and Colin stained the Basf to a beautiful dark bitter chocolate to match it.

Now this immaculately restored table needed collecting. Taking no chances, we hitched up our sheep trailer and took the ferry to Eday ourselves. It was a sharp, dry day with snow on Eday's heathery spine of hills. At the furniture workshop we were plied with hot drinks and shown around the most fascinating Aladdin's Cave of fine furniture. Hand-crafted pieces of oak, elm, sequoia, walnut and yew gleamed their silent beauty in rooms lined with wood carvings, leather-bound books and picture frames. Even the doors were an art form.

We had a few hours to kill before our return ferry: the perfect opportunity to explore Eday. Then we returned to load up our precious cargo and take her on the boat home. Now she stands resplendent in our kitchen, solid and sturdy and gorgeous in all her newly polished glory. Just in time for our Christmas feast.

Eday ~ *December*

The day we took the short ferry crossing from Sanday to Eday there was frost in the air and the sky was a clear, ice blue. At regular intervals milky, dark-edged clouds rolled over us and shed their burden of sleet. Within minutes the sky would clear and the weak winter sun smile down on us once more. Up ahead, Eday looked stunning. Fringed with green fields, her heathery hills wore a white mantle from yesterday's snow storms. We were here on important business - to collect our restored kitchen table from the furniture makers at Sui Generis. But we would also have several hours to explore the island before our evening ferry home. Eday, with her beautiful old red sandstone bedrock and her layers of deep, black peat and spine of heather clad hills, promised to be very different to our sandy island.

We began our tour right down south where farm fields edge onto the Bay of Greentoft. To our east a large green mound marked the spot of a 13th century Norse castle: Castle of Stackel Brae. We had planned to give our dogs a run along the shore here, but there were already two other dogs, with their humans, out and about. Busy place, Eday. So we drove on up the straight, main road in search of an empty beach. To our west rose the dark peat and heather hillsides of Eday's spine of hills: Ward, Leeniesdale, Chapel, Flaughton and Whitemaw. To our east lay the fertile farmlands. With snow on the ground and farm names like Cauldhame and Windywall I was shivering in my bones by the time we stopped at the Bay of London.

Eday can lay claim to a London Airport, so called because her almost water-logged airfield lies on the narrow isthmus of land between the Bay of London and the Loch of Doomy. This is Eday's trim waistline - a low stretch of land less than one kilometre wide (and that includes the beaches on both sides) that divides north from south. After a dog walk, we drove on north, past two chambered tombs and the Estate Mill, where the island's corn used to be ground. But there was no time to stop: we all needed food and the island's only shop would be closing in ten minutes.

Laden with goodies we bundled back into the Landrover and drove the final leg up to the beautiful Bay of Carrick. Overlooking the treacherous waters of Calf Sound and the uninhabited Calf Island beyond, the Bay of Carrick was the perfect position - sheltered, picturesque and strategic - for a 17th century nobleman to build his home. John Stewart was the younger son of the Earl of Orkney who, despite being the prime suspect in the fatal poisoning of his brother, was granted his own Earldom and given the island of Eday into the bargain. Meanwhile his hapless accomplice in the crime, Alysoun Balfour, was proclaimed a witch and tortured.

Carrick House remains to this day a large yet elegant manor house set in well kept grounds. Behind the house is the Vinquoy Plantation, a rare concentration of trees for Orkney. Originally planted with larch in 1833, rowan, whitebeam, ash, lodgepole pine and other species have since been added. What with this habitat for woodland birds, heather moorland for hunting hen harriers, short-eared owls and kestrels and breeding rarities such as whimbrel, skuas and golden plovers and sea-cliffs for seabird colonies, Eday is a birdwatchers' paradise.

The boys all wanted to go into the wooden bird hide, which overlooks Mill Loch, Eday's largest freshwater loch and home to those most fascinating of birds, red-throated divers. Locally called the rain goose, loom or loon, they are one of my favourite birds for their gorgeous plumage, haunting call and elusive nature. Unfortunately they are only here in their breeding season and spend the winter out at sea, so we contented ourselves with a read of the display board and the boys put the hide's window flaps (the main reason for their interest, I suspect) up and down a lot. I have to admit that we didn't see so much as a single duck out on the loch.

With flurries of snow swirling in the air we ran up to the magnificent Stone of Setter, a 15ft high, oddly hand shaped pre-historic standing stone. Then we ran on up Vinquoy Hill, littered with chambered cairns and tombs, and delighted in the views over to Faray and Westray. At 3.30pm the sun had vanished and the grimlins (last smidgeons of daylight) were upon us - time to sail home.

Hedge ~ *January*

It's mid-winter and it's bleak. Orkney in winter is a wind-battered, mud-splattered, harsh place to be. For any outdoor work we don quilted overalls, boots, gloves, hats and determination. This last is required for the full-bodied, head down, lean and push into the wind which is the only way to make any headway in an Orkney storm. I'm convinced that is why most old folk here have a permanent forward stoop.

We make plans, do the talking, before we go outside. Out in the full force of the weather, it is impossible to hear any conversation. Our landscape is grey and empty but for some huddles of sheep and scatterings of gulls hunting for worms in the bare soil of our fields. The neighbours' cows are away in their winter byres, our hens are tucked up in their house. Even the horses hover around their stables, popping in and out like those little wooden weather couples, in response to rain or sun.

Yet today, just when I'd rather stay in beside the Rayburn, we have to take a look at our boundary fenceline and make some rapid decisions. One of our habitat choices within our Rural Stewardship Scheme agreement is to plant just short of 500metres of hedging. Last spring the vision of a thick, leafy hedge all along our western boundary was lovely. The reality of the sheer slog of planting it is not quite so lovely and the expectation that it might grow and thrive is rapidly dimming in my usually optimistic mind.

Before going out I have some phone calls to make. First I phone our local SEERAD (Scottish Executive Environment and Rural Affairs Department - try saying that in a high wind) agricultural officer. I have to know that we have the rules of play, so to speak, correct. How many hedge plants are we required to plant per metre? What species should we use? How are we required to protect the hedge? What can we do about the inevitable weeds that will choke our delicate young root stock?

I jot the answers down. Six plants per metre, in two offset rows, are required. Any native species can be used but a single species cannot be used for more than 75% of the plantings. The idea is create an interesting habitat, not a monoculture. On further prompting I am given a list of 18 native tree and 16 native shrub species to choose from. Given that trees are pretty shrub-like in Orkney, I think we can use either list. The hedge must be protected against stock grazing and rabbits. Any stock fence has to be at least one metre from the centre of the hedge-line. So, in addition to our new boundary fence, we now need a parallel fence at least two metres into the field. To keep rabbits out, and give the young plants some weather protection, we need to stake a mesh tree guard around each.

Suppression of weeds is tricky and we have seen and heard of a variety of methods, none wholly effective. Herbicide prior to planting works for a while but is expensive. Mulch mats around each plant work until they rip or blow away. We have seen other, less commercial, forms of mulch in use here - straw, hay, sheep's wool, black plastic silage covers and even the old ripped cover from our swimming pool. I am wondering if using my huge heap of well matured horse manure is acceptable. Or does this constitute fertiliser, application of which is not allowed? Another question as yet unanswered is whether to plough and rotivate the whole length of the future hedge before fencing, planting and mulching.

Two more phone calls to make: one to a FWAG (Farming and Wildlife Advisory Group) advisor and one to the nursery from whom we hope to buy the 3000 plants we require. As well as all the questions already raised, I am hoping to gain advice about which species are hardiest and most likely to survive our hostile island environment. I suspect that the willow species will feature highly, but I'd also love to see hawthorn and buckthorn and maybe try some whin, hazel, juniper and elder and perhaps indulge in a smattering of wild roses.

I try various numbers and leave messages, but the morning goes by with no return calls. So I can't claim to know all the answers yet. But I have managed to stay indoors next to my nice warm Rayburn for a few hours, after all.

The Colonel ~ *January*

From the depths of warm downie-land I catch the monotone voice of the Radio Orkney weather forecaster. He rambles on a bit about sunny spells and occasional showers: that doesn't sound too harsh. With reports of shocking weather causing structural damage and flooding further south, we don't seem to be fairing too badly up here in Orkney. Then, in the same bored voice, he mentions the wind: south-westerly gale force eight, rising to nine later, or possibly ten or eleven. What? How can he forecast 50 - 70 mile per hour winds without even sounding remotely alarmed?

The familiar voice of one of our Orcadian broadcasters comes back on and tells us that several ferry sailings are cancelled and a red mini car has been caught in a particularly ferocious gust of wind, blown off the road and overturned. Its driver is, luckily, unharmed. Shaken but not broken, I guess. This reminds me of the story of a friend who had parked her car at Duart Castle, on Mull, while she went inside to speak to someone. Because her baby was asleep, she left him strapped into his car seat. Moments later a wind gust lifted the car and sent it rolling down the castle's rocky promontory like tumble weed. By some miracle the car came to a halt back on its wheels and the baby was not only unharmed but still asleep. I'd love to know what he was dreaming at the time.

I click on the light switch and am pleased to see that it works. Yesterday we, along with the whole of these northern islands of Sanday and North Ronaldsay, were without mains electricity as a hapless Great Black-backed gull tangled himself in wires. With our old oil-fired Rayburn for warmth and cooking and about a year's worth of candles in the kitchen cupboard, we don't suffer too badly in a power cut. Still, it's a reminder of all the electrical stuff we rely on and it's great when it comes back on.

Outside the wind is indeed getting busy. I hurry round the yard chasing rolling buckets and plant pots. While the horses breakfast I tighten the straps on their rugs, which resemble ballooning parachutes. It's just as well they are heavy beasts. On return from the school run Nic reports that the stone bridge over our local sea inlet is flooded by a huge tide and some of the sea wall has collapsed. We might be using the mud-ridden track up through our back fields before the day is out. But again, we hear of worse things from "sooth". Down in Yorkshire one friend is watching his roof tiles fall like confetti and another is boasting of her new house feature: a beech tree in the bathroom. At least we don't have falling trees to worry about up here.

Last week we basked in a warm winter sun, breathed ice-clear air and hurled ourselves down the fresh powder snow of a Swiss mountain. Nowhere could provide greater contrast to our flat, sandy, wet and windy island. We journeyed home, down from those mountains and through increasingly bad weather as we flew north over France then England, then Scotland and finally up to a storm battered Orkney.

We arrived home on a rough evening ferry sailing and re-united with our family of animals, all but one in good fettle and pleased to see us. The missing one was our dear old cockerel. A fine chap, we called him the Colonel for his outrageous bright orange uniform of plumage and the way he fluffed up his chest and barked commands at his somewhat mutinous brigade of land girls. In my note to our farm-sitters (now extending to six pages of what and when to feed to whom) I had added various warnings to the effect that the cockerel might die, the black cat might have kittens, the smaller horse might kick, the black collie might nip ankles. I was right on at least the first count.

To get into the house we had to negotiate a small moat. This is the water-logged foundation ditch for a much needed porch that we're adding to the house. With any luck the porch will be finished before the cracked and rickety door which presently divides our kitchen from the outside world, gives up its struggle and collapses entirely. As well as the comfort of an extra layer of door and walls insulating us from the elements, we will have the luxury of several square feet of new space for all those muddy things that presently trail through the kitchen - wellies, boiler-suits, dogs and children.

⌒

Brig ~ *January*

I hate to harp on, but the weather really isn't being very nice to us up here. After the hurricane force gales of last week, this week's forecast is a mere severe gale force nine, plus some wintery showers of sleet, hail and snow. Hey ho.

The good news is that our property stood the hurricane test extremely well, with only one length of guttering vanishing and one outside light falling off its bracket. Both of these were, um, due for a spot of maintenance anyway. On the worst day of the storm the island school was closed and the boys and I watched, from the safety of our kitchen, the anger of the wind as it hurled itself across our landscape. Being without trees, there is nothing that really moves on land. The grasses flatten, the fences lean and the sheep huddle. An occasional bucket or fertilizer sack tumbles along on its windborne journey. That's about it.

But cast your eye along the coastline and out to sea. That's where the action is. So we watched through binoculars and salt-encrusted windows, as hughmungous waves rose and crashed against our winding single track coastal road. The air filled with cotton white flecks of sea foam. The sea surface alternated with each onrush of wind over tide. The receding sea looked glassy black, mysteriously smooth as it ran out of our bay, gathering strength for is next attack. The incoming sea was a cauldron of massive white churning waves, rising up with fierce concentration, like some sea monster bent on revenge, as it hit the shore.

Our road, at this point, had vanished under a swirl of displaced water: I couldn't imagine that it would come out of this unharmed. At best it would be covered by the high tide flotsam and jetsam of the sea - boulders, seaweed, fish boxes and welly boots. This happens every winter to one or other of the coastal roads on the island and the Orkney Islands Council are pretty quick to bulldoze away the debris. At worst the road itself, or the beautiful stone bridge over our mini-estuary, would be broken. As it's our access road to the village, shops, school, airfield, pier and, well everything else on Sanday, this would not be a good outcome. I placed a private bet.

When I was at school in the Scottish Border town of Selkirk, way back in the 70's, a big old gorgeous stone bridge that linked two sides of the town was dramatically washed away by the Ettrick waters, flooding on their way to join the Tweed. From memory, one man and his dog were on the bridge at the time, the man being saved by his dog, in a sense, because it felt the bridge shuddering and ran ahead, causing him to run after it. I can still remember the sense of awe at the power of a moving body of water as I stared open mouthed at the gap where our bridge used to be. Such a solid and seemingly permanent structure whisked away in a jiffy. For a long time after that we had to drive a good ten miles up river to get round to the other half of town.

I dredged that from my memory just the other day when, the hurricane having abated, I took a walk around the coast road. It was still flooded so I climbed a stane dyke and followed the shore for a while, piled high as it was by a fresh load of boulders and seaweed. I re-joined the road where it rises to meet the sea wall. As predicted, it was strewn with debris. Ahead I could see the bridge (or the "brig" as it's called here), happily intact. So I had lost my private bet, thank goodness. But I could now see why there was still a huge volume of water on the inland side of the road. A good thirty feet of road - tarmac, foundations, concrete sea wall, the whole caboodle - had disappeared. At the end of the bridge there was now a drop of several feet into a fine tide rip. A cable - our telephone cable as it turns out - was the only thing still intact, draped and looped across the hole. It still works.

The council are coming out today to see what's to be done. Meanwhile I'm guessing we'll be trundling up our muddy back track for a while. It only takes us two miles out of our way. We won't get our refuse collected or our post and parcels delivered, but with the recent Western Isles tragedy weighing heavily on my mind, driving over a bumpy hill feels safer than the coast road.

Crops ~ *January*

Our 3000 hedge plants, guards, stakes and mulch matting are all ordered up and plodding their arduous route north to us. As soon as the plants arrive we'll be out planting, dawn to dusk, fine weather or foul, for as long as it takes. Meanwhile we have a wee bit longer by the warm stove and some more farm decisions to make.

Another of our Rural Stewardship Scheme (RSS) agreements is to undertake one area of "extensive cropping" and another of "unharvested crops". The former sounds like a good old fashioned farming practice, the latter sounds pretty damn weird. What's the point of planting a crop and then not harvesting it? Both are, in fact, designed to provide vegetative cover and feeding areas for birds. Skylark, linnet, reed bunting, twite, hen harrier and short-eared owl are all listed as beneficiaries. I'd like to think that the odd corncrake might drop in as well.

In the unharvested crops department we can choose to sow a cereal mix (including at least one legume) this spring and then leave the crop to grow, seed, get eaten by birds and, (I'm guessing here), fall over during the winter months before ploughing the remains back in next spring. Or, and I like this better, we can inter-sow two crops this spring, one of which will seed in the first year and one in the second. This means leaving well alone for two growing seasons. To the human eye this hectare of land is going to look quite messy by the end of two growing seasons of no pesticides, no harvesting and no ploughing. But to birds it should become a haven of tangled vegetation and ripe grain.

Our RSS bumf gives no specific indication of what crops are acceptable or indeed what will be most successful for the avian cause. There's an underlying assumption that, as folk with a farm, we will just know what to plant. Given that the crop is not for us to harvest and use as either animal or human fodder, it might as well be the ideal mix for birds. I phone our Orkney RSPB office and scribble down the wealth of advice and helpful suggestion that I am offered.

The first thing I learn is that there is a standard RSS unharvested crop cereal mix, available from our local seed merchant. This is a tasty melange of oats, keeper kale, linseed, quinoa, mustard and Phacelia. These last two plants produce copious quantities of, respectively, pollen and nectar: perfect for attracting our rare Great Yellow Bumblebee. Addition of red clover to the mix also acts as a green manure, conditioning the soil.

A two year mixture needs to include a higher proportion of kale or neeps. These grow large to provide shelter for birds in the first winter then go on to flower and seed in the second season. One idea is to plant half our hectare with a one year crop and half with a two year mix. This provides both early and late cover and a range of foraging areas - the magical mosaic habitat, which may even attract a corncrake. In subsequent years we can then plough the next half hectare strip along and plant one and two year mixes alternately. With this ongoing cycle any birds who have been attracted to the area won't suddenly find themselves deprived of either cover or fodder.

This addresses a potential problem for us. As a "low input" system - we don't have lots of cows to provide muck for spreading and we don't plan to apply shed-loads of fertilizer - our unharvested crop cannot be repeatedly planted on the same patch of ground. We should, instead, integrate it with our extensive cropping regime on a rotational basis to maximise the condition and fertility of the soil.

Our 1.5ha earmarked for extensive cropping is, by luck or judgement I can't remember, alongside the unharvested crop hectare. So we are well set up for all the rotational, extensive, unharvested cropping regimes under the sun. Well, the shy and not very hot sun of this near-Arctic archipelago at any rate. Deciding which harvestable crops to grow will take us at least another week by the Rayburn.

~

Neeps ~ *February*

As I was packing up my Edinburgh belongings, nearly four years ago, to head north and begin my new island life, a very urbane friend (who grew up on a farm) commented that she would be watching for signs of change in my outlook. Whatever did she mean? Apparently talking about the weather too seriously constituted an early sign of trouble. Knowing the difference between breeds of sheep was a moderately bad sign. But the point of no return, on the urban to rural journey, was when turnips became a part of your life. Definitely her most hated vegetable, the sight and smell and taste of turnips ruined her whole childhood, or so she had me believe, and summed up the horror of life on a Scottish farm. No wonder she now lives in a city centre.

Well, it's taken four years, but here it is. I'm a turnip convert. Within our Rural Stewardship Scheme (RSS) agreement we have allocated a 1.5 hectare field to a prescription termed "extensive cropping". This week's farming-for-beginners conundrum has been what type of crop to grow. The ideal behind this prescription is to encourage the cultivation of crops which will provide cover and food for birds and can be sown and harvested at times of year that cause a minimum of disturbance to their nests. The term "traditional cropping rotations" in our instructive RSS booklet sounds rather quaint, but doesn't give any leads, to us novice farmers, as to what we should plant. Another key phrase notes that the rotation should comprise "spring cereals, root crops and fodder rape". Well that narrows it down for us, but we are still unsure.

I phone three people. A very helpful person at SEERAD (Scottish Executive Environment and Rural Affairs Department) gives me the low down on what we can and can't do. She explains that the traditional extensive cropping system on an Orkney farm usually involved a three year rotation, two years of a cereal crop (oats or barley) followed by a root crop. This last would most often be neeps. (The Orkney "neep" is actually a swede or a Swedish turnip, hardier than our British one.) The need for rotation - as any good gardener will know - is to avoid disease, especially the nasty club root that all types of brassica can get.

Our local seed merchant has more information for me. We could grow kale or rape and, rather than harvesting the crop, put our sheep in to eat it in the autumn. Both provide a good finishing feed for lambs - i.e. the extra nourishment fattens them up nicely for market. But, he warns, the crop should be strip grazed, using temporary electric fencing to control access, and the sheep should always have access to a grass field as well. Kale, being the hardier of the two, lasts longer into the winter months and is probably preferable.

Neeps, he says, need a finer tilth to grow and the use of a precision seed sower (and expensive piece of kit) removes the laborious process of thinning. Neeps, he adds, have to be sown between the 15th and 28th of May. Sow them too early and they may bolt. And the 28th of May? Well that's Martinmass Day or Term Day. In the good old days of traditional Orkney farming the year was divided by two Term Days - the 28th of May and the 28th of September. On these days workers were paid and got the chance to move on to pastures new. Land tenancies were scheduled to start and end and any crops had to be in, or harvested.

For the cereal crop barley is probably the best bet up in these northern maritime climes. It also provides good feed for sheep, hens and horses. But we'll need a combine to harvest it and a barley bruiser to render the grain palatable. And then there are the traditional Orkney crops of bere barley and black oats to consider. I feel a whole new field of knowledge lurking and decide to stick to the root crop research for this week.

My third call is to a farmer. Grow neeps, he says, no contest. They grow easily, make great winter feed for the ewes and you can either let the sheep graze them in situ or harvest them as needed. And then there's the culinary delight of clapshot - an Orkney speciality comprising a happy mix of mashed tatties and neeps the like of which would leave my city friend in a clammy heap on the floor. I have to admit that I quite like it. It reminds me of stovies, especially if the cook has been generous with the butter and pepper.

Miles away ~ *February*

A gentle dusk is falling, motes of darkness filtering through the calm evening air, dimming the light of day increment by indiscernible increment. We park at the seaward end of Loth pier, reversed in to the sea wall, and step out to join the quiet gathering. Mums and Dads hover around teenagers juggling rucksacks and day packs as they greet their friends. Teachers tick off names on their clip-boards and smile reassuringly at everyone and no-one. Younger children dip and dive around legs, caught up in the emotions of the moment, yet glad to be held back by their parents.

The ferry, we could see as we drove down the last slice of land before the pier, has already left Eday and is slipping through the calm waters of the Sound toward us. In a very short time now, our precious cargo will be boarding her and sailing off to unknown adventures abroad. For, after all the planning and organising and fund raising that both teachers and community have pulled together on, this is the moment when our island's secondary school pupils set off on their trip to France.

This is not, on the face of it, an unusual event. Children all over Scotland go off on school trips on a regular basis. But consider the impact on this very small (around 600 at the last count) island population, and on the island's only school (just under 100 pupils aged between three and 16) when 24 of its teenagers are away. A high proportion of the island families have children or grandchildren or cousins on the trip. Three teachers and the school secretary are away too. That's a big chunk of our community, all of whom will be sorely missed for the next two weeks.

We have spent the weekend, like all the other families I'm sure, reading the copious, instructive notes sent round by the teachers in charge of the trip. We have laid out sets of clothes, rushed to last-minute wash a favourite sweat shirt and struggled to find enough pairs of matching socks. I'm proud to say I even got out the mending kit to darn two holes. What I cannot manage is to get used to the idea of my baby being all grown up enough to go away abroad without me. Miles, of course, is a completely sorted thirteen-year-old: organised, assured, excited yet not too nervous. He'll be fine.

The group have an arduous start to their journey. This evening ferry will take them from our wee north isle down to Kirkwall. There they stay in the Grammar School hostel, setting off early for the 6.30am Stromness to Scrabster ferry. Next comes an eight hour train journey transporting them from Thurso, all the way down the east coast of Scotland to Edinburgh. Another night in a youth hostel precedes the final leg of their journey: a flight to Paris.

Last week I asked one of the kids going on this trip if he had ever been abroad before. It turned out that he had not only never been out of Scotland, but he had never in his life been on either a plane or a train. I'm guessing that he's not alone in this. It's going to be a big, action packed, trip for them all.

What I have to do to get through this time, bereft of my eldest boy, is to cram my days with activity. The solution arrived in a large crate a few nights ago: three thousand hedge plants. Before starting what promises to be a momentous planting exercise involving sore knees, aching backs and numb fingers, we spend a day unpacking the crate. Nic and our tractor fork-lift the whole thing into our hay byre so that we can store the plants in a dark, sheltered place while they await planting.

The crate has arrived swathed in a tough version of cling wrap. We peel this off to reveal three huge bags of bare root willow. Underneath are numerous black bags filled with cell-grown plugs of nine varieties of hedge plants. We lift them out and set them carefully along the end wall of the byre. They are mostly about a foot tall, well branched and show the first suggestions of buds and leaves. They look strong and healthy and bursting with a desire to grow. Seeing them suddenly makes the hedge project plausible and exciting again.

Ne'r shed yer clout

~ Spring
2005

Dig 1 ~ *February*

Our coastline is an ever-changing contour, defining these slender Orkney islands amidst the great grey ocean. Every slight alteration to the route of a current, the highs and lows of the equinoctial tides, the building of a new pier or sea barrier, all these things can chip away at or silt up a stretch of coast. It is a dynamic process, consistent only in the fact of its constant change, mostly unremarkable and yet often significant in its medium or long-term impact.

A big winter storm, however, can have sudden and dramatic impact on our coast, taking great chunks out of the gentle slope of a beach or heaping hefty rocks up onto a grass field. Extreme examples include the "storm beaches" to be found on both Rousay and Westray, the latter being a great boulder beach, 400 metres in length, seven metres in height and five metres deep along the top of a 13 metre high cliff top.

At the other extreme, the sea can cut away at rock-solid cliff faces, chiselling majestic gloups, caves and geos and leaving behind cathedral arches, vast rock pool cauldrons and elegant sea stacks. One of Orkney's most famous coastal features, the 137 metre sea stack known as the Old Man of Hoy, is in fact the remaining leg of a two-legged stack and arch. As handy historical proof, it was sketched by an artist named William Daniell in 1819 before a severe storm destroyed one leg, causing the arch to fall.

In Sanday's gentler landscape wind-blown sand has formed inland beaches, machair and dune systems. To my surprise I have learnt that the north end of our island was, as recently as 1750, mapped as a series of small rocky islets joined only by spits and bars of sand. Blown sand has since filled in the gaps to form the single island that we recognise today. It doesn't take much imagination, especially after our recent storms and huge tides and with climate change and sea level rise a constant feature of world news, to envisage the lower parts of this island submerged below the sea once more. It is, perhaps, a judicious time to buy a boat.

On a smaller scale, a good winter storm can throw up or expose interesting things. It's always worth a walk along the coast just to see the new layer of boulders or examine the clear-cut stratification of a freshly sliced bank of land. Down at our beach field we have a completely changed aspect. At one end we now have a mountain of beach pebbles and seaweed where we used to have sand and our water channel and sluice is blocked and buried without trace. We'll need a JCB to sort that. At the other end the sea has scoured away rocks, sand and grass to expose a skilfully built sea wall, made of vertically placed flagstones, wedged together on a 45° slope. I can't be sure when it was built, but I'm very glad it's there as it has certainly prevented further sea encroachment on this occasion.

All over the island folk are out inspecting the storm damage, finding out how their sea walls have faired and scanning the beaches for treasure amongst the newly washed up jetsam. Everything from the useful: lengths of wood (pit props, telegraph poles, railway sleepers), fish-netting, oil drums and fish boxes, to the aesthetic: pebbles and driftwood, will get dragged up the beach and taken home. It's important not to take other people's finds. Anything lifted clear of the high tide line belongs to someone else. They may or may not have tied a piece of binder twine around it as added identification.

And then it's always worth staring just a wee bit longer. A family who live right across the road from a rocky stretch of shoreline went out, after the big storm, to inspect their sea wall for damage. They found their beach looking oddly altered and, after a good stare, realised that the oddity was in the pattern of the slabs of stone. The very edges of a stone kist of some sort had been exposed by the sea. Orkney has a saying "scratch the surface and you'll find something of archaeological interest". After a big storm archaeologists are run off their feet inspecting ravaged coastlines. This find has caught their interest - it might be a burial site and with another series of high tides due, it's a race against time to find out more before the sea carries the whole lot away. The site is being "dug" as I write. I'll let you know the findings.

Miles home ~ *February*

This is the perfect day. The sort of day that pushes all those mucky, bleak winter days to the furthest reaches of one's memory. The kind of day that makes this wee, remote, wild and sandy Orkney island the most perfect place to live. I'm lying on my back gazing into an intense cornflower blue sky, fringed with wisps of white cloud and lit with the fresh yellow of an early spring sun. The only sounds reaching my ears are of waves gently lapping on the shore and birds singing their, "all's right with my world" songs.

Skylarks fly high to hover over their claimed territories and sing their hearts out. A skein of greylag geese honk overhead, powering north almost to the coast of North Ronaldsay before curving around and returning to Sanday. A practice run for their northerly migration next month. A hundred yards away a hundred common seals are hauled out on the sun-warmed pebbles of our beach, while a host of waders and ducks busy themselves along the shoreline. I know this because we had our flask of coffee down there earlier. Our resident merlin is on a fencepost fifty yards inland, soaking up the sun and seemingly dozing too.

I am lying on a bed of green mulch matting, my head comfortably supported by the rolled up portion. A light easterly breeze cools my face and will lull me to sleep if I stay here much longer. But this is just a short break in the day's work: I'll have to raise my aching limbs in a minute. Meanwhile this is a moment to savour: we have planted one thousand of our three thousand hedge plants and we can tell now that the seemingly impossible task is, after all, achievable.

Our hedge planting days haven't all been like this. We have, quite literally, been out here come hell or high water - or both. With several layers of warm things plus a top layer of waterproofs on it is possible to work outside all day in gale force winds, driving rain and blizzards of face-stinging hail. You can even persuade yourself it's good for your soul, and the warm afterglow when you get home at the end of the day, peel off your sodden and mud caked gear and take tea by the Rayburn, is definitely worth the effort. But a day like today beats all that, hands down.

Our expertise as hedge planters has improved by leaps and bounds since our first clumsy effort whereby we managed to plant six willows in two hours. During this morning's slick operation two hundred plants have been heeled in, mulched and tree-guarded. First we roll out and staple the mulch matting together, thus ensuring that it is as straight and taut as possible. Then I cut six small, staggered holes per metre and Nic pushes down the dibber, creating a plug sized hole in the soil beneath. I pop the damp, root-riddled plugs of the cell-grown plants into each hole and heel them in. Finally Nic secures a tree-guard over each budding stem.

So far we have planted birch, alder, hazel and dog rose like this. Willow, being in big, straggly bare root form, involves me getting very earthy under the mulch mat. We still have whitebeam, hawthorn, sea buckthorn and a few ash and sycamore to go. Another ten days at today's rate and we'll be done. Afternoons are taken up with gathering loads of our old fence posts and laying them along the edges of the mulch matting. Whether this will be enough to prevent the whole lot flying away in a high wind is debatable, but it has already survived a north-westerly gale force nine, so I'd say its chances are good.

The other source of my contentment is that our son Miles came home, safe and well and full of good stories about his school trip to France, a few days ago. He returns taller, more assured and with a new light in his eyes. He's ready to travel more and wants to take up outdoor pursuits. He has an interesting variety of career ideas - more than I ever did. I can see him flexing his wings and taking small pre-flight jumps like a fledgling eagle. I only hope our wee island nest can hold him for a few years yet.

Dig 2 ~ *March*

Saturday is taxi day. We have three boys, each with a full schedule of music lessons, swimming sessions, sports tuition or competition and a need to see friends outwith the bounds of the school day. Living, as we do, half way along the tail of this skinny, dragon-shaped island, a trip to anywhere and back will put ten miles on the clock. I always try to work the drop off and pick up times of all these activities into some kind of "round trip" with notions of dropping off one boy "on the way" to or from another venue. But it's nonsense really: the island isn't round and there's only one road along each limb, so there is no circuitous route.

Today is the exception that proves the rule. We can drop off Miles for his half hour fiddle lesson, take Dale to his friend's farm at the North end, see a man about a dog, visit the newly exposed archaeological site, collect Miles and get home again within an hour and without retracing our steps. This is thanks to the fact that the North end road loops around our largest fresh water loch - North Loch - and rejoins the main island road further west. Excellent dude. The first three missions successful, we park by the shore and skip over sea boulders, large and small, to reach the site of last week's archaeological dig. Exposed by the recent storms and high tides, this site was first noticed by the family who live across the wee road from the narrow stretch of stony coastline. Thinking the stone cist might be a Bronze Age burial site (1800 - 600BC), Historic Scotland funded an immediate dig of the area. Unfortunately, funding constraints prevent every find from being investigated further, but the possibility of human remains pushes any find to the top of the archaeological priority list.

I have visited the site three times now. First there were merely two slabs of stone jutting out of an otherwise normal looking beach profile. Without prior knowledge I could easily have walked on by without noticing anything untoward. On day two of the dig I met the half dozen dedicated "diggers". Muffled up in warm things and waterproofs against the biting wind and sleet, they were down on hands and knees with small trowels, patiently digging and scraping. What was emerging was a beautifully crafted, bath sized, rectangular flagstone box alongside a rounded, seemingly bottomless, stone structure. Neither human nor animal remains had been found.

By the end of the dig it had been concluded that this wasn't a burial site, but that it more closely resembled a settlement feature called a burnt mound. The stone cist was probably a tank, used by filling with water which was then heated up by throwing in a succession of stones heated in nearby fires. The rounded bottomless structure turned out to be a well and parallel slabs of flagstone indicated a fairly sophisticated supply and drainage system. Most burnt mounds are characterised by heaps of discarded, broken firestones, ash and blackened earth. None of these indicative materials were found at Meur, but, squeezed as it is between the shore and the road, it is easy to imagine that they have either been washed away by the sea or remain buried under the tarmac.

On our third visit the archaeologists have gone and the site has been left exposed, for all to see until such time as the sea yet again buries it under silt and beach stones or perhaps washes it entirely away. There are many more awesome archaeological finds across Orkney, but there's something about this one that raises my heartbeat. Something about it's raw, fresh exposure, its accessibility and the knowledge that people lived here, rather than being buried here, gives the area a dynamic aura. There are no interpretive boards, no restrictive fences or sheets of Perspex bolted protectively over. There is nothing to dull or distance the pulse of life here. We perch on flagstones fashioned like a bench seat above the water tank and imagine our Bronze Age neighbours sat exactly here, chatting at they watched their water boil.

We run our hands along the top edge of the tank and find the worn dips where other, older hands have been. We look up at the nearby house and realise that there has probably been a dwelling here throughout the intervening thousands of years. Family after family after family, farming the land, fishing in the sea and, initially, cooking or bathing (depending on your view) in this water tank. I think that if I lived here I would be sorely tempted to fill this tank with water and once more heat it with fire-crazed stones. Personally I would bathe in it rather than cook in it. I hear outdoor hot tubs with a view are the "in thing".

Spring - *March*

March is known for her wild unpredictable weather and this March up here in the Orkney Islands is proving to be no exception. As spring wrestles winter to the ground and winter fights back with a vengeance, we have days of warm, tranquil beauty rudely interrupted by ferocious hail storms and biting winds. In our garden, snowdrops and crocuses nod their pretty heads delightfully in the spring sunshine, before being cruelly decapitated by winter's blast. The delicate buds and tiny, furled leaves of the hawthorns and sea buckthorns of our newly planted hedge are arrested in their development by the frigid air.

Over the past month we have accrued several interesting bird sightings. Nic and Dale came back from our wetland one day reporting two Whooper Swans and two smaller swans, also white with yellow and black bills. By the time I looked they were gone, but we have cautiously labelled them Bewick's swans, sporadic winter visitors from Siberia. Thinking that they might have flown up to North Loch we took a drive up there and scanned the cold blue-grey ripples of fresh water, flanked by swathes of winter marsh grasses. About 60 Whooper Swans graced the waves, but none stood out as different in any way.

A day later, driving round the Otterswick coast road, I caught the gorgeous pale biscuit colour of a young Glaucous Gull out of the corner of my eye. As usual I had forgotten my binoculars, so, after a quick pause to stare at it and compare it to two loitering great black-backed gulls, I scooted round to the Sanday Ranger's house to let him know. He immediately grabbed camera and binoculars and vanished. Within the day both photo and confirmation of my hunch had reached me. We have since had three sightings of an adult Glaucous Gull, easily identified by its powerful soaring flight and uniformly creamy-white plumage, over the coastal fields of our farm.

An additional pleasure of this time of year is the lengthening days. It is now light until well after 6pm, which gives us time for an evening walk. Tonight we choose the huge sand sweep of Newark Bay. A cold southerly wind pushes us back as we wend through the yellowed grasses of the dunes, hints of green growth at their base suggesting the proximity of spring. The beach is pristine, untouched by human footprints, cleansed of seaweed and rubbish by a scouring tide. Ivory sand drifts and ripples with the wind, strewn with bleached shells and sea-smoothed, pale grey pebbles. The ocean is a fast flow of aquamarine cresting to pure white sea-foam, pushed on shore by a relentless wind. A pale orange sky meets its deeper blue in a perfect, clear horizon, while steel grey storm clouds loom above.

A lone raven charts our course along the beach. Fulmars gun the waves. Oystercatchers fret and pipe, always just ahead of us. As we follow the narrow, muddied coastal track, a field full of lapwings and golden plovers rise up to look, then swing down again to resume their grassland forage. All birds we would expect to see, but no less beautiful for that.

Through the grimlins we drive home, spotting a short-eared owl in her silent evening hunt across the marshlands around our newly mended coast road and bridge. By the time we have suppered and bedded the boys, the sky is clear and starlit with swathes of merry dancers adorning her northern horizon. Last thing at night we walk up our track to get a better view of the ever-changing colours and shapes of this Aurora borealis. The North Star shines bright and low, seemingly back lit by a spectrum of greens: emerald, lime, verdigris and jade. A metronomic pulse of white light repeatedly breaks the dark horizon. This is not part of the natural phenomenon of the Northern Lights, but a fitting accompaniment: the North Ronaldsay lighthouse, flashing her warning message.

We walk on through the cold, indigo night air until, in a sudden flurry of wings, our silence is broken by a flock of ducks as they lift up from their roost and become silhouettes against the weird green sky.

Piglets ~ *March*

Seven year old Fenning could be, in the nicest possible way, described as mildly eccentric and comes up with some pretty whacky thoughts and ideas. So when I ask him to consider what we should get Nic (Dad) for his birthday, I should be prepared for the unexpected.

"A piglet" he says, without so much as a sliver of hesitation or a chink of doubt. Now where on earth did that idea spring from? We did watch that pig friendly and super-whacky film, "Babe" at Christmas, but that was over two months ago. My reactive laughter is taken as agreement by the boy and the next thing I know I'm looking up pig breeds on the internet and getting excited by the thought of all the rough, weed ridden corners of the farm that a pig could tidy up for us.

To be honest, although Fenning's suggestion came out of the blue, I have been harbouring a growing notion that we should have a pig or two here. Every time I browse a Smallholder magazine or flick through the Farmers' Weekly there seems to be a wee article (never a big, front pager) on pigs and what a useful addition to the farm animal community they are. Since deciding to investigate further, I have found a wealth of information via the British Pig Association, the various rare breed trusts and the many individuals around the country who keep pigs and have been happy to share their knowledge and enthusiasm with me. In a very short space of time I have gone from pig-ignorant to pig-interested and from thinking we might get one, bog-standard pinkish weaner to wanting a breeding sow from the selection of rare breeds available.

The pig's merits are many-fold. They will eat virtually anything - household scraps, vegetables, grass, weeds, roots and cereal crops. Thus they will clean, plough, rotivate and fertilise land for you to subsequently cultivate without any of the sweat or machinery usually needed for all of the above tasks. Meanwhile they have converted all of that waste matter into either prime pork or compost. With the help of some moveable electric fencing I should allegedly (I'll let you know) be able to contain the pigs in the various corners of weed-ridden land that we have, until such time as they clear it and are ready to move on. On reading the glowing descriptions of each of our British pig breeds, I cannot help but notice how often "escapism" is mentioned. Whatever pig breed I am reading about it is always billed as more docile and less likely to escape than all the other breeds. Pride in one's chosen breed notwithstanding, someone has to be wrong!

Intensive pig farming, where the animals are kept indoors and in confined spaces, tends to give the pig a bad image involving smelly muck and unpalatable swill. But many of the rare breeds, of which I have discovered about a dozen, are hardy, outdoor types, who will apparently thrive even in this cold, northerly Orkney island. They are also great characters with, to quote the Middle White Pig Trust, charm and personality individual to each breed. To the unpractised eye, colour is the main feature distinguishing the different pig breeds. The pinkish white flesh of the Middle White, Large White, British Landrace and Welsh pig is contrasted by the darker shades of the Tamworth, the Berkshire and the Duroc and the stripes and spots of the Saddleback, the Hampshire and the Gloucester Old Spot. Scanning the printout of thumbnail images of pig breeds, my eye instantly alights on the glossiest, the biggest and the darkest - the Large Black. Now there's a beast I would like to have around the place.

On further investigation it seems I have not been unwise in my choice. The Large Black is, according to the blurb, extremely docile and very hardy. Its dark skin renders it less prone to sun related skin problems and its long ears obscure its vision to the extent that it doesn't easily escape. I feel rather sorry for it on the latter score, but anything that reduces the chances of a pig escaping across the island has to be considered a good thing. In the end however, for all my research on and enthusiasm for the rare breeds, it proves too difficult to get a piglet from the nearest Large Black herd in time for Nic's birthday. I settle for ordering a Large White weaner from a reputable pig farmer on Orkney Mainland. He has a litter ready for weaning three days before Nic's birthday. In a final burst of madness I order two - I wouldn't want these gregarious animals to be lonesome.

Islanders ~ *March*

Islanders (assuming the island is remote and the population small) are probably among the best multi-taskers in the world. There are usually more jobs to be done than people to do them. Within a population of five hundred, minus the children, the elderly, the infirm and the unwilling, there aren't that many people left to do everything that needs doing to maintain a community of human beings.

There's the school to run: teachers, cooks, janitor and cleaners. We have four shops and three post offices, all fully staffed. Then there are pier masters, airfield stewards, hauliers, bus drivers, council workers (mending roads, collecting refuse, clearing flooded ditches etc) builders, electricians and plumbers. There are two pubs, a tea room and a take-away, B&B's, a hostel and several self-catering cottages all to run. Every community needs an ambulance driver, an undertaker (the same person in our case), a fire fighting crew, a doctor and nurses. Our swimming pool needs lifeguards and maintenance. On the social side of life, there are clubs to run: youth, music, dancing, sport - the community calendar is pretty full and for each event there are several multi-taskers behind the scenes. And then of course there's the farming and fishing that underpins the whole of community life here.

It becomes harder to describe someone who has a many-faceted lifestyle. In the Hebrides we used to know people by their job - John-the-post, Archie-the-pier, Iain-the-pub and so on - even though they were all crofters with their own land and animals as well. One such was Mary Fish, who drove the fish van. She had been known as Mrs Fish for so long that when she became ill and was admitted to hospital, no-one could recall her real surname.

I've been multi-tasking a bit myself over this past week, although I wouldn't rate myself among the champions. As a mother, housekeeper, potter and writer who is also rapidly turning into a farmer, I had the daft notion that I could fit in a four-day, swim-teaching course. Billed as easy and interesting, I put my name down for the course last autumn, when life wasn't quite so busy. By the time the appointed four days arrive I have gained several more animals (more feeding and mucking out), I'm living in a building site (constant washing of mucky clothes, footwear and the house floors) and I am also committed to a Sanday Fiddle Club concert on the final afternoon of the swimming course, with a rehearsal the morning before. Then I catch sight of the course schedule, which appears to involve being classroom bound 9am to 6pm with some evening pool sessions and homework thrown in. This could be tricky.

Ever the optimist, I decide I can do it all. I get up earlier to feed all the animals and finish the "homework" that I didn't manage the night before. I practise my fiddle when I should be emptying the washing machine or sweeping the floor or writing. The boys get better at finding their own clothes, swim/gym kit, music and food in an increasingly chaotic house. Nic manages all the cooking and the boys' taxi service, whilst also fencing, farming, concreting and squeezing in intermittent moments on his real job - running a business in Yorkshire. Whenever I glimpse him in his tractor cab he always has a mobile phone pinned to his ear.

Into the midst of all this arrives my mother, on a ten day trip to see us. I can only apologise to her for the fleeting glimpses she catches of us as we whizz back and forth, and say thank you for all the casseroles she saves from cremation in the Rayburn.

This evening is the final day of Mum's stay. It seems everything is done. Fiddle concert, swimming course, fencing, the day's building. The horses and hens are fed and tucked up for the night. I can see our sheep, into the final six-weeks of their pregnancies, contentedly munching grass or taking a turn at the mineral lick out in the front field. The dogs are snoozing after a hard day running after the tractor. Could we, perhaps, relax, drink wine and catch up on each other's news? A phone call from the ferry puts paid to that idea in a jiffy. The piglets have arrived and we need to meet the trailer in Kettletoft to off-load them.

Telly ~ *April*

Last night I received a phone call which completely changed my plans for today. I had been going to paint our newly completed porch - sand yellow for the walls, white around the windows and, finally, sea blue for the concrete floor. All of my signature colours, repeated throughout the house, to remind me of my favourite places in the great outdoors. Once effectively stranded outside the house I was going to spring clean the horses' stables and tidy up the garden, in preparation for my green-fingered mother-in-law's visit next week.

"There's a BBC2 film crew on the island producing a programme about Sir Peter Maxwell Davies and his involvement with the Sanday Fiddle Club and community. They need a 4x4 to get them along the rough tracks. Can you lend them your Landrover or even drive them around for the day?" It transpires that the crew got their car stuck in the mud the first time they ventured off road. Perhaps not the right folk to entrust with my vehicle, but it might be fun to be their driver. Despite several days of mist and rain, the forecast bodes well and it's been a while since I drove around our beautiful island for no particular purpose other than to admire its fabulous vistas. It's mad, really, to take a day out from my endless "to do" list. I say yes.

Dawn seeps through lingering wisps of mist and the rising sun burns off the damp air to reveal, at last, a true spring day. A clean, fresh aura pervades the island. The grass is greener, the sea is bluer and the sky is clear of those dark storm clouds that have hung around all winter. After an early start to feed animals and pack children off to school, I meet up with a delighted film crew - yesterday's weather had shrouded the whole island in a secretive mist and left them bewildered as to quite what they were meant to film.

After an extensive loading operation - these guys have a lot of kit - we set off. I have a mental list of the many picturesque places that I would like to take them to. We home in on Start Point as a good place to begin, not really so much for its name as for its extreme, wild beauty. I drive through Lady Village and out along the fringes of Cata Sands, across the Plain of Fidge and finally around Lopness Bay to where the tarmac ends. We bump our way along the pale sand track and park at the old stone boat house, overlooking the fast tide rip that cuts us off from Start Point.

Cameras, tripods, sound equipment and an assortment of bags and boxes are unloaded from the back of my landrover. The men are quiet, each focused on his particular set of gear, only exchanging necessary queries and instructions. As cameras roll, a total hush descends and the air fills with the swell of the sea, the buffeting onshore breeze and the singular calls of gulls.

I look around me. It's so long since I did this. It's one of those ironies of life that, even in this most beautiful of places, one forgets to make the time for such simple pleasures as just sitting on a beach boulder and breathing in the pure air. I walk quietly down to the pebble beach and sit on a sun-warmed rock, my muddy farm boots digging in to sea-scrubbed shell-sand. I contemplate my surroundings as if through a camera, using my thumbs and forefingers to mimic a frame, landscape or portrait. The blues of sea and sky layer over and filter through each other with infinite intensity. White sea foam breaks onto seaweed strewn black rock. A seal bottle-bobs five yards offshore and fixes her liquid-brown eyes on the camera crew.

Familiar territory takes on a new veneer. Old tree trunks of driftwood, swathes of dead dune grasses, pebbles strewn across pale-gold sand, the old wooden doors of the boat house: all become an art form in the presence of a camera. I shift my position to find the perfect spot: sun on my face, yet sheltered from the fresh breeze. Curlews pipe their lonesome story all along the shore. Down in a grassy marshland two oystercatchers probe the wet tilth with their strong yet sensitive bills while lapwings flip and tumble like circus acrobats overhead. I'd like to point out all these gorgeous birds to the crew, but they look so engrossed in their silent work that I don't interrupt. I'd guess they're getting some pretty glorious footage.

Pregnancy ~ *April*

Over the past four seasons here I have kept a handful of sheep and we have limped through lambing with a combination of luck, help from our neighbouring farmers and my ancient memories of time as a student nurse on the obstetric wards of the Western General Hospital in Edinburgh. Now we have 68 ewes most of whom look healthily heavy around their middles. It really is time I learnt how to do this lambing thing properly.

If I've got my dates right, our lambing is due to begin in the first week of May. The exact sheep gestation period varies with breed, but a range of 142 to 154 days can be relied upon. We put rams in with the ewes on the 13th of December and they certainly got on with their task with admirable efficiency and gusto: our first lambs could arrive anytime after the 3rd of May. That's assuming all our ewes achieve full term pregnancies and don't succumb to premature labour, prolapse, abortion or any of the extensive list of nasty sounding diseases that I have spent this morning reading about.

There's pregnancy toxaemia (also known as twin lamb disease), chlamydiosis, vibriosis, toxoplasmosis, hypocalcaemia and ovine progressive pneumonia, to name but a few. Problems occur via either poor nutrition or a variety of vicious and persistent viruses, bacteria and parasites. All in all there's an awful lot can go wrong with a sheep at this time of year. In fact from one text I read that around 70% of both ewe and lamb deaths occur at or close to lambing time. We could put our flock in to graze a minefield and expect a similar rate of loss. There is only so much book reading one can do on this most practical and applied of subjects. I want to talk it through with someone. The trouble is, our local crop of born and bred farmers seem to find it hard to explain the rudiments of sheep husbandry to me. I think the problem lies in the fact that they know so much, and have been doing it for so many generations, that they have no concept of how little I know. They cannot think of what to tell me because it's all second nature to them. So I decide to turn to two different sources.

Firstly, I phone our veterinary surgery in Kirkwall, only to discover that our vet is out here in Sanday today. That's brilliant, if I could only catch up with her. I leave various messages which I hope will reach her ears before she takes the islander flight back to town tonight. Then I phone a couple on the island who I happen to know have also recently bought a wee flock of sheep and are in the middle of their first lambing season. I know that their lambing dates are a month ahead of us and I know that they will have researched the subject and prepared for the event thoroughly. I know all this because they are the folk to whom I sold my lovely old farmhouse and they are an extremely organised couple.

I set off for a nostalgic trip back to my old house. The track is neat and already lined with newly planted Rosa rugosa hedging, the yard is freshly gravelled and devoid of all the weeds, limbless action men, punctured footballs and badly parked bikes that I used to have to negotiate. My old veggie patch is freshly dug over and sports a fine greenhouse. And the end byre, which we used as a dumping ground for odds and sods many and various, has been transformed into an exemplary lambing shed. Fresh straw and clean feed and water troughs grace each well made pen. The byre's old double doors are propped open onto the sheltered back field. A fridge and cupboard hold medicine and equipment for every conceivable eventuality.

We lean over the end gate and watch their hefty ladies-in-waiting whilst contemplating the ins and outs, the highs and lows, the successes and the failures of our sheep farming experiences to date. I fill several pages of my notebook with thoughts, ideas and things we need to buy before our confinement begins - you can't really go anywhere once lambing starts. By the time we've run through all the potential birthing problems our conversation inevitably turns to what to do with the failures. Illness and death, it seems, are never far away from sheep and all us shepherds can do is protect our flock from the nasties that we know about and maintain a sharp spade, a designated burial ground and a sanguine attitude for everything else. The vet appears just as I get home, with the excellent news that she's running a one day lambing course this Wednesday. Perfect. I get straight on to our inter-island airline and book myself a day trip to Kirkwall.

Antenatal class ~ *April*

I'm sitting in one of the veterinary surgery's treatment rooms, listening and watching as our vet pulls an interesting array of items out of a large blue plastic crate. Me and four other trainee shepherds are an hour into an intensive, one day lambing course. Our tutor (Kate the vet) has already run through flock profitability, ewe condition, nutrition, vaccination and gestation in a rapid-fire, clear and concise monologue. It's fascinating and urgently needed information, yet I can already feel my brain reaching overload. I hope I can take the pace.

The blue box is the lambing kit. By the time it is empty I have a list of twenty two items, all of which I need to source and take home by the end of today. There are the menders and the revivers: anti-biotics, glucose, calcium, dopram, artificial colostrum, with their required syringes and needles, drenches and catheters and gastric tubes. Some medicines are given by injection (subcutaneous (under the skin), intra-muscular or even intra-peritoneal (straight into the abdomen) some by mouth (via a tube or a drench). Other bottles contain iodine and a variety of antiseptic washes and scrubs. Everything: you, the sheep, the byre and the implements, need to be kept as clean as possible to avoid some of the nasty ills that can afflict a sheep at lambing time.

Next come what I guess could be called the lambing aids. Although they sound pretty horrible, they are used to help and ease the lambing process. These are the ropes, the snares, the restrainers and the retainers. As Kate holds up each item and explains its use, my mind flicks back to my days as a student nurse, consigned to the labour wards for four weeks. Remembering all the frightening looking forceps and other weird implements available to help deliver a human child, I can't help but think that lambs have the better deal.

The ropes, used to secure lambs' legs and pull them out, are of a lovely soft material a bit like an old school tie (in fact I'm sure you could use a couple of ties, if you happened to have them to hand). The snare, designed to be flipped over the lamb's head and behind her ears for the final pull out, again looks soft and comfortable. The restrainer is simply a moulded piece of plastic that holds the ewe's head and forelegs still, enabling you to concentrate on the job in hand at the other end. And the retainer? Well OK that one's not quite so pleasant a prospect. I won't go into details here, but I'm sure you can imagine.

Once you have your lamb, or lambs, you need towels to give them a good rub dry (I have a stack of old terry nappies lurking in my airing cupboard, which will do the job nicely). If they don't immediately suck from their Mum then you need to provide them with colostrum for their first 24 hours of life and if for some reason they are orphaned then powdered milk, a whisk and teats and bottles are essential. I jot down "kettle" as another essential in the lambing byre. Hot water and towels are, it seems, ubiquitous to all maternity units. A really cold lamb (a thermometer is pulled from Kate's box of tricks) may need to go into a lamb warming box. This is the equivalent of popping them into the warming drawer of the Rayburn and is usually a home-made affair involving scrap wood and a fan heater. Another warming device is a heat lamp strung low over a small pen (a gunnel). Everyone in Orkney seems to call these "piggie bulbs", an allusion to their use for litters of piglets in the good old days when every farm kept a sow.

Over a welcome cup of coffee, the lambing box is cleared away and another box, sloshing with warm water, hoves into view. This is the artificial ewe, complete with real pelvis through which we are going to spend the rest of the day thrusting our arms. Notepads are put to one side and overalls donned as we prepare to get down and dirty.

Several hours later we have all successfully delivered lambs presented in every position from normal to breech to completely upside down and back to front. We have talked through everything normal to abnormal, pre to post lambing. We have had a go at docking and castrating - using those tiny, tight rubber rings for both - and at giving injections. It has been a full-on, fast pace, instructive and enlightening course, which I would recommend to anyone who ever needs to help with lambing.

Missed boat ~ *April*

I'm on the boat home when it happens. Something I didn't think possible. But then I am the sort of person who would assume it wasn't possible, or right, in the great scheme of things.

Nic and I have taken the ferry to Kirkwall more times in the past fortnight than ever before. This is because Nic's stalwart and generous Mum has made the arduous journey from Yorkshire to Orkney to hold the fort for us. To date, whenever Sue has visited, we have scarpered south to sunnier climes (Aberdeen, Inverness, Edinburgh, nowhere too exotic you understand) to relax and indulge ourselves in luxury hotels, urbane wine bars and funky restaurants. This time, given the opportunity to head off unhindered by children and the trammels of school timetables, we couldn't think of anywhere we wanted to go. This could either be construed as proof of our love of the idyllic bliss that is our adopted island life, or an alarming symptom of our increasing insanity as we get drawn into this all consuming occupation called farming.

Foremost in our minds at the moment are the farming tasks, many and various, which have to be undertaken in the next few months. There's lambing (sixty odd ewes due to lamb during May), ploughing, sowing, fertilizing, harrowing, mowing and baling, to name the most obvious tasks. In order to complete these tasks we need, first, to go shopping, big time. We need a whole heap of machinery, ironmongery and tools. We need animal feed, crop seed and fertilizer. We need a new set of boiler suits and steel toe-capped boots and tough gloves. We need, all told, several trips to our mainland town to source all this exciting new (and second hand) stuff. Having never been much of a shopper, I've finally discovered my niche - hardware and machinery shops are my favourite.

Today we have been taking a long slow look at a topper. It's one of those machines one doesn't immediately appreciate the need for. It cuts higher than a mower and, we now realise, will be invaluable for keeping the weeds at bay across our grass fields. As I walked across our back field the other day all I could see were emerging docken plants. We do a deal on the topper. Then my eye is caught by a complete sheep handling system: holding pens, forcing pen, race, footbath and shedding gate. It's one of those things one stares at with admiration for a while and then (when told the price) rapidly decides one can build oneself.

So, we're out on deck on the boat home, after one of our shopping days. On the car deck below us our Landrover is laden with galvanised steel sheep troughs and hurdles. Fifteen minutes out of Kirkwall harbour we're already savouring the prospect of catching up with the boys and Nic's Mum as we settle in to steak, salad and a good red, when it happens. Our ferry suddenly spins, as if on a sixpence, through 180 degrees. What on earth is happening? Engine failure? An emergency illness of a member of the crew or passengers? World War Three? We can't think what would cause our regular-as-clockwork ferry service to alter her course.

The Nord Star, a cargo vessel who has been delivering tarmac to Sanday, is suddenly very close to our starboard and we briefly wonder if we've had a near miss. But two passing crew members quickly relieve us of our bewilderment. We are, believe it or not, going back to Kirkwall to collect a late passenger.

Now there's not much that riles me. But someone who arrives at the port after their desired ferry service has departed, and then makes enough fuss for the good-natured ferry captain to turn back for them, someone who causes me and all the other passengers and crew to be nearly an hour late getting home, well that riles me. Whether it's a bus or a train or a ferry or a plane, if you arrive too late then you've missed it. You've missed the boat, mate.

In this case it's only through the good will of the Orkney Ferries staff that this man gets his boat home. I heavily suspect that, rather than setting a precedent, this incident will cause a whole slew of new rules, involving checking in early, purchasing tickets in advance and so on, to come into play. It's a shame when a perfectly good and understandable system is abused. But there's nowt so weird as folk.

Seed merchant ~ *April*

We park at the back of the shop, between a fork-lift truck and a stack of palettes. Through thick slices of heavy-duty plastic curtain we enter the realms of William Shearer, Seed Merchant, Kirkwall, Estd. 1857. On the ground floor is an array of gardening tools, compost, growth enhancers and weed killers. I trip over a rake and then remember that ours broke last week. Nic tucks it under his arm to buy.

We choose four of the biggest plant pots available: we have two tiny oak saplings and two equally miniature chestnut trees, which need a cosy home to begin their life on our windswept Orkney Island. They hail from an ancient woodland in Yorkshire and will need all the help they can get.

I'm eyeing up the front of the shop, enticed by a range of old-fashioned, white enamel kitchen ware, when Nic suddenly lopes up a set of time-worn wooden steps that I had not noticed. They look like the staircase to a hay loft or artist's garret. I follow and enter a different world. The space is entirely wood-clad. Floorboards have the dull gleam of wood polished by the feet of a thousand customers, swept and scrubbed by generations of seed merchants and their sons. Roof rafters and beams glow in shafts of honey sunlight filtering through skylights. Two huge wooden desks sit at right angles to each other, delineating a central space. One has a sloped surface, like a teacher's desk or the lectern in a Kirk.

I find Nic weighing himself on a massive set of scales. The dial swings round further than he would like and he jumps off quickly. Thirteen year old Miles has taken to baking irresistible lemon drizzle cakes and it's not good for our waistlines. The scales are set to zero with an empty bin on the weighing plate and I watch as our seed merchant deftly scoops in a variety of grass seeds until he achieves his desired mix and weight. Then, in a surprise move, he tips the seed onto the bare floorboards and gives the whole pile a good mix through with a long-handled, shiny metal spade. He might be stirring the ingredients for a giant's bread loaf, but instead he shovels the mix into a hessian sack before deftly unrolling the top and cotton-stitching it closed with an implement resembling an oversized stapler. This is our dose of "seed screenings": a low cost mixture for patching our field gateways.

All around the room are similar sacks, some stitched, some open with their tops rolled neatly back to reveal their contents, some of traditional jute hessian and some of the more modern, woven plastic equivalent. There is seed stock in this room for every crop a farmer could hope to grow in our northern climate. Oats, barley, grasses (rye, timothy, fescue and cocksfoot), clover, herbs, kale, rape, turnips and peas, to name but a few. Any combination of seed can be mixed - usually in a huge hopper at the end of the room rather than on the floor - to provide the ingredients required for anything from a grass sward to a silage crop, a beetle bank to a bowling green.

We are here to collect our order of seed for a five acre horse hay field. The recipe includes a tasty mix of ryegrasses, creeping red fescue, smooth stalked meadowgrass, a wee bit of white clover and some herbs - burnet, yarrow, parsley and ribgrass. It is destined for our corner field, a beautiful headland of sandy soil bordering our beach. We'll sow it in the next couple of weeks and hope it grows well in the summer sun. Richard consults his big old leather bound ledger, which has permanent residence on the master desk. I can see our farm name at the top of the page, followed by a list of items and quantities, neatly set out and hand-written in a timeless, flowing script. He ticks off the grass seed order then sets off round the room to collect up the other sacks. Unharvested crop mix, oats, barley, peas and neeps. This last is handed to me in a small brown envelope, folded and selotaped. We're only doing one acre of neeps, but I still expected a larger package than this. I guess they start very small and grow very large.

With all our purchases loaded onto a palette, a high reaching fork-lift suddenly appears at the edge of the loft floor (I wouldn't want to bring a toddler up here) and whisks our wares away. By the time I get downstairs our landrover is full to the brim with seed sacks. This seed merchant's mission statement reads, "Quality and tradition for today's farmer" and I do feel that that's what we've got.

~

Buds ~ *May*

They say that one swallow does not a summer make, but it's enough for me. Seven-year-old Fenning first saw it from his favourite bird-watching spot - our trampoline. He will sit there for hours some days and then come into the kitchen, pour himself a glass of milk and plonk at the table to flick through the bird book muttering descriptive details about legs, bills, feathers and tails. Often he draws the bird he has been watching. He's not a list maker (yet) but the birds he knows he has seen from his trampoline include starlings, blackbirds, skuas: arctic and great, herring gulls, redshank, shelduck, short-eared owl, raven, oystercatcher and now, swallow.

Hardly your average garden birds, but that's the beauty of a coastal garden. When I first got interested in the watching and identifying of birds (a skill I have to admit to being fairly sloppy and inconsistent about) I lived in a tiny cottage perched on a rocky promontory with heathery hills as a backdrop. The first birds I came across were divers, sea ducks, gulls, waders, buzzards and eagles. I'm still very vague about all the passerines (LBJ's or little brown jobs, as they are known in the birdy world) that flit around proper gardens.

Another sign that summer might almost have arrived on this northerly outpost of Orkney is that the grass is, at last, growing. Throughout April's ghastly weather any hope of a spring like warmth in the air was quickly dashed by a Siberian gale force wind or a torrential downpour. Our yard alternated accordingly between sand swirling desert and mud bath. I seem to remember describing our March weather in a similar vein. Orkney weather is like that: relatively mild winters, but one helluva haul to achieve a level of warmth one could call spring. When spring does, finally arrive, it is explosive, dramatic and stunningly beautiful.

So our fields are finally greening up. I read in the Farmers Weekly a good couple of weeks ago that farmers in the depths of England were whipping off an early silage cut. At the time our grass swards were an estimated inch long with the sickly hue of plants that hadn't seen enough daylight. The farmer's calendar is clearly quite different in Devon than in Orkney.

With such evidence of spring all around us we plucked up the courage to walk the length of our 500m hedge. After all the finger and knee-ache of planting it, I hadn't dared look to see if it was surviving. But we have been blessed. Green buds are emerging all along the line of saplings, with rosa rugosa, hawthorn, sea-buckthorn and whitebeam taking the lead over birch, sycamore, willow, ash and hazel. Interestingly, the plants we put in first, way back in mid-February, are no further forward than those we planted last, a good six weeks later.

We now know why farmers here are to be seen whizzing around on tractors at the first whiff of good weather. There's a lot to do in a very short season. And just when the fields need ploughing, rotivating, fertilizing, seeding, harrowing and rolling, the cows start calving and the sheep start lambing. Life gets busy. On our own wee farm we now have four of our ten fields ploughed, one for tatties, one for a new horse hay meadow, one for our Rural Stewardship Scheme unharvested and extensive rotation crops and one because it's lying fallow and Nic wanted to practice his ploughing skills with his newly bartered (i.e. extremely old and found in someone else's farm yard) three furrow plough.

This morning I wake to a brightness of sun edging our black-out blinds the like of which I haven't seen for many months. I get up and walk out along our front track with the dogs. It is 6am. Sunshine fills the air, skylarks sing their hearts out up in the clear blue heavens, gossamer spider webs silver the damp grass and ground hollows hold vestiges of a dawn mist. Swallows flit and swoop on increasing numbers of flying insects. Cattle and sheep graze contentedly in the stillness and silence of this most glorious of mornings. It only takes one day like this for me realise what a paradise we live in. But I'd like a few more, please.

Birth - *May*

I'm on location, writing to you from the breezy outpost of our lambing shed. A laptop computer is a wonderful gadget, especially useful when multi-tasking. This morning, as well as writing, I am on watch for the arrival of more lambs.

Seven days ago we brought our pregnant ewes in from the fields and ever since we have kept them in the lambing byre by night and let them roam the yard and wee paddock by day. We've had a sweepstake running as to who will drop her lambs first and the boys picked out two huge girls as their favourites. So sure were we of their imminent labour that we put each in a single pen, ready for their happy events. Seven days on and no offspring have issued forth from either.

Meanwhile in one of our two communal overnight pens all is quiet at the five a.m. check but by seven a.m. there's a minor scrum of half a dozen ewes all laying claim to one cute little girl lamb. We move cautiously in and Nic protects the lamb from stamping hooves while I start eyeing up back ends to see who's most likely to have given birth. We've just sussed who it is when Nic spots another lamb, safely curled up in the hay rick. We lift him out and "mum" seems happy to have both so we pen the three of them up and watch as she licks them clean and nudges them gently round to her teats. Once both have successfully sooked, we feel pretty happy that we've put the right parent with babes.

But it's a bit of a lottery. Short of the unfeasible options of either separately penning each ewe, or watching over them every minute of the day and night, there is the chance of a mix up. We have been warned that, especially with an experienced flock, one birth will awaken the mothering instincts of several other ewes. The danger is that a ewe will happily take on these newborns and then abandon either them or her own, when she delivers a few hours or days later. The unobservant shepherd can end up with an awful lot of unclaimed lambs, which then need to be foisted onto another ewe or else bottle fed.

We're feeling lucky. Our first newborns are feisty, quick on their feet and feeding well. Mum delivers her afterbirth on cue and stamps her foot protectively whenever we come close. We iodine their navels, weigh them and, proud parents that we are, video them: the first lambs to be born on this farm for many a year. I wake the boys and they tumble out of bed, into clothes and out to the lambing shed as fast as their sleep-fuddled heads can manage, bent on being first to see our first lambs. Then, knowing she is waiting for news, I phone my Mum.

Now we are reluctant to leave the byre unattended, lest we miss someone else going into labour and aren't so lucky with the outcome. We have furnished the byre with an extended confinement in mind: fridge, kettle, chairs and a lovely old roll-top desk, presently housing everything from the castration bands to the flock record book, my half of our walkie-talkie set, my laptop, dictionary and several coffee mugs. Nic has even rigged up a capacious Mexican hammock for overnight duty. Once I have finished writing I'll probably fetch my fiddle and see if a little rhythmic number or two doesn't bring on a fresh batch of lambs.

We've been told a few good Orkney Island farmers' tales recently, the funniest of which is that a rain storm brings on the lambing. I say funny with deep irony because we have had nothing but blasting wind and torrential rain for the past week and it doesn't appear to have advanced things. In fact, without meaning to harp on about the weather yet again, I do feel compelled to mention that I am still wearing the same padded boiler suit, woolly ear-warmer and gloves that I was wearing in December. So much for the notion of scheduling lambing for the warmer month of May.

One down, sixty-seven to go. I'll keep you posted.

Flying ~ *May*

I'm up in the sky, flying high over Scotland, and she's looking particularly beautiful in her Spring garb. Colourful chequered tablecloths of farm fields fill the spaces between the rooftop dot matrices of rural towns and villages. The verdant green of silage fields and the citrus yellow of rape crops are stitched around with the verdigris of unfurling hedgerows. Coppices cling to knolls and tall trees grace the roadsides, the only land to have escaped the plough.

We fly north, over the fertile plains of Stirlingshire and Perthshire. Broad rivers snake, silent and cool, along their well-worn routes. Hills rise above the farmland mosaic, draped in the fawn brown of pre-flowering heather. Scotland's Cairngorm Mountains reach up to the sky, folded and cut through by upland streams hurtling their waters down in to deep, cold lochans.

A wall of cloud looms ahead. After two days of sunbathing in my parents' garden in Perthshire, here is the forecasted weather front. Our pilot announces our descent toward Inverness Airport and we plunge into the thick whiteness, the landscape below obliterated in an instant. I shut my eyes and mind to the turbulence and only open them again once I've felt the bump of our wheels hitting the tarmac beneath us. The more I fly, the less I like it.

While we're grounded to deliver folk to Inverness and pick up those destined for Kirkwall, Orkney, I sneak a look at my text messages. The latest one from my hubby, Nic, reads, "2 prs. 1 breech, 2M+2F all OK": a very similar message to the many that have arrived before it.

I have only been away since Friday night, but in the intervening 48hours I have missed the arrival of a third of our lambs. As predicted by the "sods' law" maxim of life, our lambing was going quite sluggishly in the week prior to my brief trip away, but speeded up somewhat the moment I left. Nought to sixty in two days. Every text message since my departure has involved the arrival of twins - in many cases several sets at once. Night or day, rain or sun, lambs have been popping out all over the place. I reckon my husband and sons might be quite tired by the time I get home.

We lift up and out of Inverness and before the cloud envelopes us I catch sight of the Beauly and Moray Firths looking grey and choppy, and of the coastal farms, sandy green grasslands sprawled across with the mustard yellow of gorse. Then I settle in to my book, accept a Bloody Mary from the drinks trolley, and try to relax until we once more hit land, this time the bonny lands of Orkney. At Kirkwall I disembark with my only hand luggage: my gorgeous new fiddle nestling in her as yet unscuffed black case. I wouldn't normally travel with it but, with a music exam tomorrow I needed to keep practising. And in a way I was also playing for my parents, to celebrate their golden wedding anniversary.

I share the airport bus into Kirkwall with a nice lady from Edinburgh, who turns out to be my music examiner. She is travelling all this way north to put eighteen of Sanday's many musicians through their paces. Another text message heralds the arrival of more lambs at home. I still have an hour and a half on the north isles ferry before I reach home and can be of any help. The bus drops my fellow passenger at her hotel (she is sailing out to Sanday tomorrow) and then takes me down to the harbour. Through a blast of icy evening air I board the ferry and take the stairs down to the cosy canteen: I need a mug of tea and a bacon roll before I brave the elements up on deck.

There's an odd lack of text messages while I slip through the north isle channels and sounds to Sanday's pier at Loth. I am met through the 10pm darkness by a harassed and dishevelled Nic and three sleepy boys. They have been rushing to settle the sheep for the night, deal with two more births and try to catch one of our Jacob sheep, who has lambed out in the field. As soon as we get home I chivvy the boys to bed, whip on a boiler suit and head out into the wind and rain to help Nic get the Jacobs in: it's not a night fit for a newborn to be out.

⌣

The final straw

~ Summer

2005

Fee ~ May

Missive two from your own correspondent, on location in a lively lambing shed on a wee farm in Sanday, Orkney. It is two weeks since I last wrote to you from here and the scene is very different. The ten individual sheep pens behind me are all full, each mum with at least one lamb, most with two and one with three. Our two nursery pens each have five families, all looking ready for their next change of venue - out to pasture. By my feet is a cute wee girl called Fee. She is our only "caddie" (orphan) lamb at the moment, and she thinks I'm "Mum". Her real mum didn't die but only had one working teat, which was dominated by a larger, bossier sister. Her name comes from "Feed me" which is what I was going to spray-mark on to her back, only I ran out of room.

It is only fourteen days since our first lambs were born and we now have 105 lambs successfully up and running. Fifty-seven of our sixty-eight ewes have lambed and we have reason to believe that four of the remaining eleven are not pregnant. Phew, only seven to go.

Twelve lambs have taken the lonely road to our designated burial site. As the old saying goes, where there's livestock, there's also deadstock. Being born is a dangerous time for a lamb. The first problem is getting out. We have been lucky with a good proportion of normal deliveries: that's head and front feet first. But we have also had a sample of all the other pictures in our lambing guide: breech (bum first), head first but with one or both front legs stuck back, legs first but with head back and mixed up twins. I am so glad I went on a lambing course before all this started. All the deliveries we have had to assist with have resulted in live lambs.

The next challenge is to thrive in the big bad world. Even a nice cleanly bedded lambing pen is, by definition, colder and muckier than the womb. Suddenly there's a need to get to one's feet and find a food source. A good ewe will lick her lambs until they are cleaner and drier and nudge them in the direction of her milk-filled udder. A good ewe will also protect her lambs from danger. Unfortunately we've had one newborn trampled by over-enthusiastic mothers-to-be in the communal ladies-in-waiting byre and one triplet lain on to the point of suffocation by her own huge and rather dopey mother.

For the most part we keep the families in for a day per lamb i.e. two days for twins, three for triplets. On day two they get tight rubber rings applied to their tails and testicles and have numbers sprayed onto their sides: red is for singles, blue for twins and green for triplets. Then they go into one of our nursery pens for a day to check that each family is well bonded and the lambs are feeding well before we chivvy them out into the field.

The exception to this routine is our Jacob sheep. The first gave birth while still out in the pre-lambing field and we chased it into our sheep trailer for shelter. Next up was a gorgeous set of triplets which we managed to pen for a day before mum saw freedom through a high open window and jumped clear out. When our third Jacob mum evaded penning by jumping over me, her horns and hooves combing my hair on the way past, we realised that these are wild and hardy beasts, not meant to be trapped into confined spaces. We now have two sets of triplets, one set of twins and three singles all roaming free in six acres of grass. Of all the newborns these Jacob lambs have been my favourite. They emerge wriggling with energy and a determination to succeed. With their slender necks, steeply sloping foreheads, long snouts, budding horns and enquiring eyes they look for all the world like baby dinosaurs freshly out of their pre-historic eggs. Their black and white spotted mantles make them hard to spray numbers on to - even in this they don't conform to flock protocol. By way of improvised identification we have given each a pattern of multi-coloured dots, crosses and stripes.

From my desk I can see our back field dotted with grazing sheep, sun and sea air helping their lambs to grow and thrive. As shelter from the inevitable rain and wind we have put out rows of straw bales. Lambs run round them, playing hide and seek and stand on top to be king of the castle. Gambolling lambs, what a pretty sight.

Art ~ *June*

At last. Sunshine, and an excuse to abandon the lambing shed for a couple of hours. My sister and her family are here and I want her to meet a friend of mine. We leave the boys (old and young) with our newly sown hay field to roll, a handsome bronze cockerel weather vane to erect and a quad bike to whizz around on. As we bump up the back track Jean spots a young lamb stuck half way under the field fence. She texts the news to the boys and before we lose sight of the farm we can already see the lamb being lifted free and returned to her Mum. Sometimes mobile phones can be handy.

To reach my artist friend's house we head for the north end of Sanday then turn briefly inland, away from her southern and toward her northern shores. From Dominique Cameron's garden, the elegant sweep of Sandquoy Bay stretches before us, an arc of aquamarine ebbing and flowing up and down a swathe of pale gold shell sand. You can't live much closer to the sea than this, garden and ocean divided by no more than a rocky bank and a dry stane dyke. I'm dwelling on the inspiration such a vista must give an artist, when my thoughts are interrupted by a yelp of recognition. Dominique and Jean have, it seems, met before. Years ago in Edinburgh. I guess I shouldn't be surprised. Small country, Scotland. Small world, Earth.

Coffee and catching up complete, we repair to Dominique's studio for an early preview of her latest paintings. Across the lawn from the house is a lovingly renovated old boat house, the gable end of which is pure glass and the beach side of which has a long, narrow landscape shaped window. Through the low doorway we enter a realm of calm whiteness. Daylight streams through the windows onto a white-painted wooden floor and as yet unpainted plaster-board walls. It's like walking into a blank canvass. A large dark-wood easel dominates the centre of the space, keeping company with a smaller, metal music stand. A square wooden table is laden with tubes of paint, pots of brushes and colour streaked rags. All around the edge of the floor are boxes of paper, rolls of canvass and baskets of paint. A dimple radiator stands, unplugged, waiting to be useful. Dominique's fiddle slumbers in its case. The landscape window perfectly frames the bay.

The paintings I'm so keen to see are stacked on a sofa, faces to the wall, as yet unframed. Dominique turns them and flicks through them. I catch glimpses of familiar island land and sea scapes, flashes of colour. Skies of iron grey, cobalt blue or storm yellow meet deepest blue horizons and aquamarine seas. Coastal grasslands of yellow ochre and raw sienna mingle with the blacks and browns of a rocky shore. Flecks of white cloud or sea spray uplift the intensity of colour. Hazy suns shed light across wild seas, wind-burnt grasses and deserted beaches. A distant lighthouse or a remote cottage give a reminder of our minimal human presence in this wild, dynamic spit of an island lying in the merciless arms of rough oceans. The paintings are in stunningly vivid contrast to her monastically plain studio.

I ask, somewhat disingenuously, about the inspiration for these paintings and get a thoughtful answer. This windswept island landscape is laid bare, stripped back, edgy, harsh yet precarious. There are no trees or mountains to soften the scenery or to distract the eye from the naked, wild beauty of the place. It is a fitting reflection of living one's life on this remote island. Undistracted by urban facilities life here is also stripped back and simplified in a way that can be tough, while also fabulous. One is forced to become more self-contained, more introspective and to find one's own rhythms. It is a challenge that she admits gives her infinite inspiration for her painting.

As Dominique describes how she walks through and revisits a landscape repeatedly before she paints it, I am reminded of our resident composer, Max (Sir Peter Maxwell Davies) who describes how he composes whilst walking the length of a beach. His composition is so linked to his environment that, in order to revisit a musical phrase in his head he has to retrace his steps up the beach. Studying my friend's paintings I can feel the wind, sun or rain on my face, sense the time of day, the freshness of the morning or the calm of the evening and be fairly sure that I'm alone in this isolated place. They admirably reflect the island that I love.

Pub Lunch - *June*

The other day Nic suggested going out for a pub lunch, just for a change. It took me a moment to comprehend his meaning - I haven't been out to a pub since forever. We have two pubs on this island but, although I'm sure that they are both fine establishments, we just never think of going. So I was intrigued by Nic's sudden enthusiasm and further bemused when I overheard him phoning Orkney Ferries.

To reach our pub lunch we were, it turned out, taking our Sanday to Kirkwall ferry then driving across Orkney Mainland to the north-west ferry port at Tingwall to board a wee ferry bound for Rousay. By leaving our house at 8.30am we could reach our lunch destination by midday and be home again by 6.30pm. Not so much a lunch, then, but actually a whole day out. One of my husband's dafter notions.

At Kirkwall we say goodbye to eldest son Miles, who is taking part in a fencing tournament (involving foil and sabre rather than post and wire). At Tingwall we join the queue of three cars bound for Rousay and hop out to stretch our legs and watch the MV Eynhallow plough through the churning currents of Wyre Sound. I suddenly feel like a tourist, despite still being in Orkney. We pull out into a slate-grey, choppy sea. To our left are the hills and vales of Mainland topped by the three wind turbines on Burgar Hill. On our right lies Gairsay, a privately owned island, her cap of heather moorland set at a jaunty angle over her green slopes of farmland. Ahead is Rousay, an impressively high lump of land, her uplands disappearing into cloud. A low lying green foreground gradually separates from Rousay as we sail closer. This must be Wyre, a mere slip of an island, and the higher ground beyond must be Egilsay.

On closer inspection Rousay's steep coastal slopes are terraced - the result of glacial retreat. There's a clear demarcation between the fertile lower slopes and the peat and heather covered uplands. On the map the contour lines are packed tight to represent this steep rise of land to a series of inland peaks, plateaux and high, fresh-water lochans. I have already decided that we must come back this summer for some leg work through those hills. For today there is precious little time. Upon landing in the sheltered wee harbour we are facing the Pier Restaurant and Pub. We park next to an ancient Fergie (tractor) and pile out. The pub lives up to all my expectations and memories of such dens: oval wooden bar, plush vermillion upholstery with matching wallpaper, pool table centre stage and scampi and chips on the menu. We play pool, eat and I drink a rare pint - a fine lunch out.

One of Rousay's claims to fame is her endless road, said to be the longest road in the world, because it is a single loop, with not so much as a give way sign to spoil the flow. We set off in a clockwise direction and, being tourists today, we drive slowly, hesitate to consult our map and meander into passing places. Along the south west side of Rousay is Westness Walk. Known as the most important archaeological mile in Scotland, this is simply littered with cairns and settlements dating back to Stone Age, Iron Age, Viking, Earldom and Clearance times. We only have time to visit one or two sites today, but again the map is enough to make us want to come back soon for a longer visit.

We chose the most obvious site - Midhowe - and park and run down the steep path to the coast. Ahead is a large Nissan hut type building and I'm wondering why all the signs are directing us toward a farm byre when Dale and Fenning shout, "it's inside!". Sure enough, within this vast building is the incredible "Great ship of Death", a stone age cairn within which remains of Unstan pottery, many animals and twenty-five humans were found. We walk along aerial walkways to look down into the twelve burial stalls of this 23 metre long structure.

Then the boys are off across a grassy precipice. They have spotted an even more amazing structure: the Midhowe broch, a large and intricately built Iron Age dwelling. Set on a grassy knoll above a coast of giant flagstone paving, decorated by sea-pinks and delicate lichens, this is a most fascinating of sites. We all love it and it's hard to drag the boys away, but we have the rest of the island to drive around within our remaining thirty minutes. The north side of Rousay is gorgeous, but we have run clean out of time. We haven't done this beautiful island justice and will return for sure. But we have had our pub lunch, our mad day out. That was good.

Concrete - *June*

As I write I can hear the lovely rumble of a not too distant concrete mixer warming up for its morning's work. I never thought I'd say this, but I have grown to love concrete. It is the solution for muddy yards, weed-ridden garden paths, wind-harassed corners and rodent infested houses.

Our yard has been a quagmire all winter, albeit partly because it has been host to all the building and concreting materials needed for our new porch. Now the porch is complete and we are in the final throws of circumnavigating the house with a concrete path - thus filling in all those holes through which mice and rats can access the wall space. The path also means (hallelujah) the boys can get from house to trampoline without muddying their socks (wearing boots for such a short trip is deemed too much hassle).

I know some natural flagstone or fancy cobbles would have looked much nicer, but these things are hard to get hold of and expensive to transport to remote wee islands. Concrete works. We can mix it on site and pour it wherever we want. We can build walls on top of it (around the house and to keep sheep, dogs, hens and wind off the garden) and we can set the few flagstones we have found around the farm into it, to make a haphazard garden path. We can use it to anchor fence posts and strainers and we can use the leftovers to shore up the somewhat shoogely perimeter of our dog kennel and to block off any suspiciously rodent sized holes around the base of the byre walls.

Another traditional farmyard material I have learned to love is binder twine - that orange or sometimes blue, or even pink, string used to tie hay and straw bales. To be found in every nook and cranny of any farm near you, it is both the most annoying and the most useful of things. It hangs in bundles off those ubiquitous six inch nails banged into the roof timbers of every farm byre in Scotland. It gets trodden into winter mud around hay ricks and along tracks and appears to grow up with the Spring grass, to be pulled and pocketed in idle moments. Indeed, a length or two of it loiters in every farmer's pockets, handy for tying up a broken fence or dragging exhaust pipe. String and a penknife is the perfect pocket mending kit for most things around the farmyard.

To set up lambing pens we bought a whole consignment of metal hurdles which ingeniously link together. One hurdle lifts into the foot of the next, which then has to be lifted over the top of the first. It's easy enough until you have a series of them all relying on each other for support. Then lifting one becomes a hassle. Tying them with binder twine, however, is quick, reliable against a restless ewe and makes use of all those bundles of the stuff.

Years and years ago I was shown how to stay warmer when working outside on a wintery, windy day. A farmer (I can't remember who, but maybe he can) seeing me shivering, came and tied a length of binder twine around my waist, making a tight belt around my billowing jacket. It was a fine remedy for all those nasty draughts: I remember being instantly cosier.

Our pigs - now grown large and living at large in our beach field - have a fine time playing with concrete and binder twine, both of which they seem to delight in digging up. Every morning we walk down to the coast with a bucket of feed and return with a bucket of freshly dug ancient twine. This is an excellent way of clearing the field. Slightly more alarming is their penchant for concrete. The floor of our beach hut (an old concrete building that was once used as a hen house and has now become the pig house) used to be smooth concrete. Now, thanks to the industrious work of two Large White pigs, it is half dug up, great chunks of concrete upended to reveal the soil beneath. Their zeal in this task is such that I'm beginning to wonder what is buried under there. If we find any bones I'll let you know.

Concrete and twine: these are two of my favourite things.

Fast boat - *June*

We're crossing the Lashy Sound on an extremely fast boat. Steve, the skipper, shouts to us that the combined engine power adds up to that of 450 horses and that we're presently cruising at 35 knots. I seem to remember that our north isles ferry chugs along at seven knots. This certainly feels different. Nic, undaunted by my allusion to madness with regard to our last lunch date, has organised another one. This time we have chartered the bright orange, 10 metre humber rhib, called "Explorer" from Kirkwall, enlisted enough friends to help us fill its twelve seats, and packed a gargantuan picnic. One thing is for sure about our Orkney Island climate: when it comes good make the most of it, get on out there and bask in it.

At 10am sharp, out of the silence of a gloriously calm and sun-filled morning, Steve zipped in to Loth pier at the south end of Sanday to collect us. His son and first mate, Marcus, in addition to the requisite survival suit, was sporting a crash helmet, complete with visor. Before we boarded, he handed up a bunch of high-tech life jackets, one for each of us. Once seated, an additional life raft was pointed out to us. Safety is paramount when crossing our northern waters in such a powerful boat.

I'm thinking that at this speed we'll be landing at Westray within ten minutes - too early for the folk we're collecting there - when the boat veers round to the right and heads straight for the cliffs of a wee island called the Calf of Eday. From a distance it looks as though there's just been a funeral: a large congregation of black-clad people are bowing their heads in earnest conversation on the clifftop. But this is an uninhabited island and these are not people but cormorants. This small isle holds Orkney's largest cormorant colony. Just when our adrenaline levels have risen several notches, Steve throttles back and we come to a serene halt under the cliffs. Sea pinks and scraps of green vegetation adorn every nook and cranny. Cormorants perch and nest on every available ledge. Sheep and this year's crop of lambs graze the precarious clifftops, venturing down onto ledges like mountain goats. The farmer must lose a few of his stock in mountaineering accidents, but his flock also has a huge colony of great black-backed gulls, which dominate the centre of this grassy island, from which to protect its young.

We chunter slowly through the Calf Sound, Eday to our left, Calf of Eday to our right. We have been through here on the ferry before now, but in this boat we're at sea level and - a bit like driving a low-slung sports car - the world takes on a new grandeur. We pass the Quarrel Geos (sea-carved ravines) and I wonder if it's the noise of the seabirds that gave them their name. Ancient settlements, pre-historic cairns, a tightly roofed shepherd's barn and the ruins of a 17th century saltworks present themselves along the coast of the Calf. A lower, gentler shoreline gives fulmars plentiful nesting opportunities. We sail within spitting distance, but the boat seems to present them with less of a threat and they don't leave their nests to attack us. Meanwhile the Eday coast is dominated by Carrick House, where the notorious pirate, John Gow, ran aground and was held captive.

At the north end of Calf Sound Steve swings his boat expertly around to the right for a closer look at the massive cliffs of Grey Head, with its protruding "Knees" and its beautiful natural rock arch. This is the domain of the guillemot: thousands of these auks cover the vertical cliff face, litter the sea below and decorate the rock with their pungent, white guano. I spot some of the so called "bridled" form - wearing thin white spectacles over the otherwise dark brown plumage of their heads. Back out into open waters we shoot past Eday's corresponding Red Head (with headlands respectively called East Toe and West Toe). Someone points out the first puffin and as we approach the cliffs of Westray we begin to see more and more seabirds - puffins, razorbills, guillemots and tysties (black guillemots). Arctic skuas and great black-backed gulls - the thugs of the seabird world - fly over and dive-bomb rafts of smaller seabirds. A lone gannet plunge dives for its dinner.

The east coast of Westray is pock-marked with geos and caves and Steve treats us to a dip into several. In one we disturb rock doves - it's only in these remote places that true rock doves are to be found as elsewhere they have interbred with feral pigeons. In another we find a seal pup, waiting desperately for his mum to return - I hope she does. Then its time to collect our friends from Westray and head out to our picnic destination: another uninhabited island.

Not cricket ~ *July*

Last Saturday the sun shone down on one of our traditional annual events: the North Isles Sports. The three largest of Orkney's northern islands, Sanday, Stronsay and Westray, take it in turns to host this event. This year it was held here in Sanday and, although none of us was actively involved, we fully intended to go along to our school playing fields and watch a few races. The competition didn't begin until after noon so we had a whole morning free to complete our farm chores.

We were up early on this fine and sunshiny morning. Everyone was fed, watered and released from their overnight quarters (hens, caddie lambs and our one remaining pregnant ewe) or brought in from the fields to the stables (my horse, who suffers a sunburnt nose on days like this). By 8am we were nursing mugs of coffee in our gorgeous new sun room (garden room, conservatory, whatever you want to call these things, it's a lovely, clear-roofed room which allows us to enjoy the sun without the wind - a rare accomplishment in Orkney). This was, we decided whilst sitting with our feet up on the table enjoying uninterrupted views across farmland to the fabulous sand dunes at Cata, a good morning to do some sheep work.

In preparation for all the things one has to do to keep a flock of sheep healthy (drenching, injecting, clipping toe nails, shearing wool, tagging etc) we had already set up our first attempt at a pen and race system in our yard. All we had to do now was round up our flock into the outer yard and process them one by one through our system.

Whoever, ever, said gathering sheep is easy (I think it might have been me). Over last winter we reckoned we'd got quite good at rounding up and shifting our flock. So, with three sons and two dogs in tow we headed out to our field of sheep with that fatal "this'll not take long" attitude which I thought we had stamped out of ourselves a good while ago. Our sheep obligingly trotted around the perimeter of the field until they got to the yard gate, at which point they suddenly had urgent business to attend to back up at the top of the field. I realised at this point that our new challenge involved the lambs who, being both clueless and mischievous, didn't follow their Mums obediently but got all muddled up at the edges of the flock. So our Mums would happily trot round the field but no way were they going to leave the field without knowing where their babies were. Ergo, chaos.

We added several sheep hurdles to the end of the open gate, making a much longer barrier with which to force them into the yard. Several laps of the six acre field later we had most of the flock in the yard and decided to close the gate on them. Lambs immediately clambered back through the bars of the gate - a cattle gate, not a sheep gate and now we appreciate the difference. The resultant pandemonium required a good deal of sprinting, leaping hurdles and rugby tackling before order was restored. We ran this half-flock through our race quickly and efficiently and shed (separated) the lambs into a wee pen of their own so they wouldn't get squashed. Then we began to put the ewes back through the race one by one, stopping them in the crush for drenching, toe-nail clipping and marking, before releasing them, via a footbath, back to their lambs. Our system was working well, with the only design fault being that Nic and I had to clamber back and forth over hurdles many times as we dealt with each part of the process. I was beginning to feel like one of those athletes who staggers determinedly through the final miles of a marathon.

Having thus processed a dozen ewes Nic called a halt for a tea break. We were weak at the knees and sweating copiously: it seemed a reasonable idea. Twenty minutes later we returned to the yard and realised our mistake. Sheep are escape artists who can push through any amount of metal hurdling given the time to work on it. Our remaining incarcerated ewes had bulldozed their way back out to the field where they happily grazed, now completely unconcerned as to the whereabouts of their lambs, who were still penned in the yard. With a deep sigh I released them and sent them on their way.

Time had slipped inexorably by and noon was long gone. We had run many miles and jumped a thousand hurdles. My voice was hoarse from yelling at our errant sheepdogs. We decided that, rather than catch the tail end of the North Isles Sports we would stay home and redesign our sheep system over a beer or two.

Faray - *July*

Imagine a storm laden night in late December, 1908. Your fishing trawler has just been driven onto the rocks of a 100 acre, uninhabited Orkney Island by the force of seventy mile an hour winds and raging seas. You can see no escape from a cold, wet death for you and your crew. But, by some miracle, you are spotted by a man on the neighbouring 300 acre island. Your next vision is of five strong men in an open boat, risking life and limb to reach you, rescue you, and take you back to the warmth of their firesides.

That is the amazing story of the Hope, a fishing vessel from Peterhead, which ran aground on Holm of Faray and whose crew were rescued by the five men of Faray. These two tiny islands are formed of a ridge of Old Red Sandstone which almost connects Westray and Eday. At the time, Faray was populated by a mere eight families. The list of rescuers is resonant with traditional Orkney family names and place names. William Burgar of Cott, John Hercus of Doggerboat, James Groat of Leaquoy, Robert Reid of Holland and John Drever of Windywall. Before I ever went to Faray I read this, and stared at the contradictory picture of the five men, dressed in their Sunday best for the newspaper man to take a photo, yet sitting on fish boxes outside what looks like a wooden boat house. So last week, on Faray for our fabulous picnic, I walked around the ruinous buildings of Holland, Doggerboat and Windywall and imagined the lives of these men and their families through dark, storm-bound winters and glorious, sun-filled summers.

Faray, one of Orkney's smallest islands, is now, sadly, uninhabited. With such a small land area, it probably never had a huge population. At the turn of the 20th century just over 50 people were enjoying the delights of this gorgeous wee island, with farming, fishing and the spoils of ship wrecks to keep them alive. Way back in 1529, author Jo Ben's description of Faray conjures up a green and pleasant land where the cows grazed verdant foliage whilst the local farm boys sang to them, corn grew abundantly and fish were plentiful in the surrounding seas.

But the early twentieth century saw Faray's fragile population decline. Two keystones to an island community - a school and a pier - were denied Faray and heralded her demise. The first was closed in 1947, causing the families of the four kids who had been attending Faray School to move away. The second was never built: when other small islands were offered a pier and a regular ferry service as a post-war bonus, Faray made the mistake of choosing a smart tarmac road to connect all her farms instead. The road remains to this day - I walked along its smooth, grassed over surface only last week - but the people have gone. The last family to leave were the Wallaces of Ness, evacuated in 1947 after sixty years of farming there.

Since then Faray has been inhabited by sea birds, seals, sheep and, briefly, red deer. A couple of years ago we were lucky enough to meet the farmer of Faray, the most singular and intrepid Marcus Hewison of Westray, who tends his flock by regularly braving the choppy waters of Rapness Sound in his trusty boat. When he needs to gather his sheep from both islands, he and his dog have to leg it across the Lavey Sound (which runs between Faray and Holm of Faray) at low tide, take on the marathon hundred acre round up and bring the sheep back across the causeway before the tide cuts them off. To take the year's crop of lambs to market, Marcus lands a small ferry, usually the Eynhallow, at the south end of Faray and persuades his sheep to climb aboard. Sometimes they have to swim a bit. Now that's what I call island farming.

Back in 1981 Marcus decided to have a go at red deer farming and duly landed eight of the beasts on Faray. His experiment was short-lived as the deer expressed their disapproval of their new home by plunging into the sea and swimming to Eday - a bracing distance of some two kilometres. I've never heard what happened to them next. Does Eday have a population of red deer?

Shearing 2 ~ *July*

That old list of things to do before you are forty should definitely include shearing a sheep. Happily, I am safe from that challenge, being nearly three years past that delightful celebration of four decades of life. But hubby Nic, still on the youthful side of that watershed, took on the task of shearing our sheep with gusto, determination and a little help from some friends.

Shearing has been one of those things on our sheep farming calendar which we knew had to happen, but which we were trying to ignore until we had mastered a few other farm skills: lambing, ploughing, sowing etc. Last week we found one of our Jacob ewes dead on her back, cause of death unknown but likely to be as simple as the weight of her coat of wet wool rendering her unable to get up. She leaves triplets, who luckily seem old enough and feisty enough to survive without her. Having had no ewe deaths through lambing, this one seemed to me to be unlucky but also unnecessary: we should have them sheared by now.

On the same day we took a phone call from our Westrayman friend, Marcus, offering - oh joy of joys - to come and help us clip. He could, he said, come to our island on his way to Kirkwall for a wedding. On my map Sanday is not "on the way" between Westray and Kirkwall, but this was no time to quibble and I sort of knew what he meant. Sometimes "on the way" can describe a time slot rather than a geographical route.

Our first task, given the dodgy forecast, was to gather in our flock and keep them under cover for a night. Clipping wet fleece is not a good plan. With all too recent memories of our sheep gathering skills, it was with heavy hearts that we set off around the field on the evening before shearing day. But this time our sheep, with a psychic clarity unique to the species, decided that the yard and byre were absolutely the best place to be. We had them all tucked up for the night within minutes. Personally I think sheep possess great intelligence and a keen sense of humour.

Our shearing day dawned fine and dry. We collected Marcus from the morning ferry and another friend, Ian, turned up to join the party. With the electric clippers rigged, two clean cow mats on the byre floor, a table (two water barrels and a door) ready for rolling fleeces and the sheep and lambs sorted (our shedding system worked perfectly this time) it was all systems go.

We watched Marcus's clipping routine intently as the first few sheep passed through his expert hands. Then it was time for Nic to have a go. I was contentedly rolling fleeces and had no intention of swapping jobs. As each successive sheep was ushered forth, Nic would learn how to clip one part (the back, the shoulders, the belly, the neck) and then let Marcus finish off. Ian worked away like a Trojan in the next stall. By midday we had half the flock resembling stunned goats and I had a nice stack of fleece and a goodly covering of lanolin up my arms.

It was time for Ian and me to be at fiddle club (we were on day four of our Sanday Fiddle Club Summer School week). As I left I looked back to see Marcus and Nic pushing the next dozen ewes through to the shearing stalls. They looked, respectively, like a man on holiday and a man after his first attempt at an army assault course. I wished them luck for the afternoon and got two wry grins in return, one brimming with humour, the other gritty with determination.

Several hours later I returned to see our main flock all shorn and out in their new field and our second flock - those who didn't have lambs this year - on their way up the beach track to the yard, Nic, Marcus and the dogs plodding behind. Ian returned and we slotted back into our routines for the final round of clipping. Nic was now clipping whole sheep, albeit sweating profusely and lying down to straighten his back out between each. As the last ewe was sent forth with her new cropped look we breathed sighs of relief and were about to crack open the beers when someone mentioned the ram.

Maggie May - *July*

I've gone and done it again. Fallen in love. Her name is Maggie May. She has a coat of bright bay, four white legs, a flowing mane and tail (except where her naughty brother chewed it), a very inquisitive muzzle and a big friendly look in her eye. At four years old she is 18 hands high (6 foot high from floor to withers and then a large head and neck above that) and towers over most of us humans. She is, of course, a fine example of that most noble of animals, the Clydesdale horse.

Clydesdales really are big friendly giants. Big on strength, they are synonymous with the term "horse power", as the traction engines that eventually superceded them in the world of work, had to be measured in terms of how many times more powerful they were than one horse. The breed was developed way back in the early 1700's along the lands of the River Clyde (now known as Lanarkshire) where a mix of agriculture and heavy industry gave them plenty of employment. To achieve the perfect horse for working the heavy soils of Scottish farmlands - powerful, yet lighter, leggier and with wider hooves than their forbears - farmers chose stallions from the original Flemish and English heavy war horses and put them to their smaller local mares. The resultant Clydesdale became increasingly popular throughout Scotland, northern England and Ireland and was exported as far afield as America, Canada and Australia.

To further promote the breed, Clydesdale stallions used to be walked from farm to farm to service the mares within their (often extensive) territories. The men who walked with them were called the staigymen (stallion walkers) and often achieved a similar reputation to their equine charges. It was a case of let out your mares but lock up your daughters on the day the staigyman arrived.

Through the decades of industrialisation and mechanisation the call for heavy horses declined and by the 1960's the Clydesdale was considered a rare breed, only kept alive by a few stalwart families and only seen by the wider public in show rings and parades. Now the heavies are enjoying a return to popularity in the horse world, for showing, driving, extracting felled trees from forests and for riding.

Clydesdales are now being hailed as a fabulous riding horse, in every field from dressage to endurance, although riding them is nothing new: our mounted police have favoured them for many years and I'm sure farmers used to hitch a ride home on their plough horses. I'm certainly a big fan of the ridden Clydesdale: they have a fantastic flowing, agile stride, manage to exude power and grace simultaneously and are friendly, gentle and biddable to boot. Having known a good few flighty arabs and obstinate ponies in my time, I would put Clydesdales at the top of my preferred horse breed list any day.

Being on such a big horse has the advantage of enhancing one's view of the world. I have spent a happy Spring riding out (albeit usually in the rain) on my first Clydesdale - the magnificent Lady Helen - and seeing parts of our island that I had previously passed unnoticingly in a car, on a bike or even on foot. Nic has been a stalwart: walking/jogging alongside, looking faintly fed up and increasingly exhausted at the rattling pace set by Helen's long, swinging legs.

For the last couple of months I have scoured the country, far and wide, in my search for another of these noble beasts, so that we can stride out together. I had even gone so far as middle England in my (online) search. Then, just the other day, a friend mentioned this horse biding in Orkney Mainland - only one island and twenty miles of water away from us. And so I met Maggie May - and have been humming the traditional version of that song ever since, "you may search from here to China/ you'll not find a girl that's finer/ that's finer than my darlin' Maggie May."

Euphemisms ~ *August*

We leave tomorrow on a week long trip sooth. As usual, I have very little inclination to leave our beautiful little island farm in these far north isles of Orkney. We'll be swapping tranquillity for traffic, space and freedom for bustle and fumes. Mind you, I wouldn't mind a dose of that warm bright thing in the sky, which has so far, mostly, evaded Orkney this summer.

But therein lies one good reason for not leaving the farm right now. As soon as we had finished shearing sheep our thoughts turned to hay making. We pencilled in the first, then the second, then the third week of July for cutting our hay field. Every time we thought about it great deluges of rain rendered the very idea ludicrous. At least we didn't rush to our mower in the brief dry spells, as we know a few folk did, only to watch the cut grass lie in increasingly soggy piles for the rest of the month.

This morning we did everything we could to prepare for hay making as soon as we get home. The mower is ready to cut, the tedder (hay bob) is ready to turn and the baler is ready to bale. We have scrubbed out our hay byre, since its last incarnation as lambing shed, and lined the floor with wooden palates, ready to take a few hundred bales of hay. We can now only hope for two things: that we don't miss a week of sun and return to more rain and that our hay crop doesn't become lodged (fallen over under its own, sodden, weight). We will, at any rate, be cutting our hay in August, which is good for the corncrakes (shame we don't have any).

On a more positive note, our beautiful coastal field, sown with a rich hay mix back in May, now has a verdant green carpet of herbs and grasses. Yesterday we moved our flock onto it for the first time. The idea is that they will trim the new grass and chomp away all those unwanted weeds during the week, and then we'll move them off it again as soon as we're home. Our sheep gathering skills took a distinct turn for the better yesterday. When Nic drove into the field on our wee quad bike the sheep made a bee-line for the gate without demure, the beep of a horn and the rev. of an engine seemingly more authoritative than either our dogs or ourselves.

Other things that are growing well include an inordinate number of thistles and dockens in our putative garden. As a gleeful fellow islander said to me: you can take a garden out of your farmland but you can't take the farmland out of your garden. Our unharvested crop, a mix of oats, kale, linseed, quinoa and mustard is looking gorgeous and I'd quite like to bale it for the winter. Our extensive crop rotation of turnips, field beans and barley is also coming along nicely and we will definitely be harvesting those. And finally, beyond our field of knee high tattie plants, our pigs romp around in beach field, now fully grown and ready for that equivocal term, finishing.

Another animal that I would definitely finish off if I only I could get my hands on it is the rabbit (or is that twenty?) who is steadily chomping her way along our new hedge. This morning I looked up rabbit control (another euphemism) and found that, alongside helpful advice about trapping, poisoning, shooting or fencing out, was the idea that one can deter the wee blighters by sprinkling the area with coyote urine. One can even have the stuff shipped from America. On an island with neither foxes nor buzzards to keep the numbers down, our Sanday rabbit population is reaching plague proportions. But I do wonder if they would recognise the smell of coyote, given that they've never met one.

The final blight on my island-scape this week is hogweed. I do agree in principal with the idea of leaving corridors of land, field edges and verges, uncultivated. The idea of swathes of wild plants is wonderful for both wildlife and aesthetics. But all that seems to grow here is great clumps of hogweed: an irritant to both human and equine skin. I do wonder if this plant forms a useful part of any animal's habitat.

Home - *August*

My holiday reading was a book about someone's house and all the people who ever lived in it. The author undertook extensive research in order to find out the history of her home. It was an interesting concept, most of all because it prompted me to think about the life and times of our home prior to our arrival.

There is one huge difference between trying to find out the history of a London house and that of an Orkney farm. While the London author poured over endless piles of archived ledgers containing birth, death, marriage and transaction documents, all I have to do is ask around. In fact, I haven't even had to do that. Ever since we moved in, folk have offered me snippets of information, usually while passing the time of day between a weather observation and some farming advice.

Of course we know the woman who sold us the property, who now lives on a nearby farm, and the folk she rented the house to for a couple of years, who have since moved to Shetland. We know the preceding farmers, who altered and extended the house considerably during their thirty-odd years here. They have retired to a house near the school, where their many grandchildren can drop by anytime. They come round for a yarn every so often, to see how we're getting on with the farming and to check out the changes we're making to the house. When we first moved in it was Jim's in-depth knowledge of the plumbing that helped us out of a sticky patch.

Of their six children, we know three - one is a postie and two drive the school buses here. A fourth is known to us by her childish announcement, "Rosie wos ere" scrawled above the old kitchen heater. And a fifth we know as one of our "Sunday drivers": folk who trundle around the island's back roads on a Sunday afternoon, just for a wee look, to see what's new.

Our boat home last Saturday took an inordinate three and a half hours. She was running at half speed, on her one good engine, and had to visit Eday and Stronsay before arriving in Sanday. While the football team became (in the nicest possible way) increasingly raucous in the lounge, Nic and myself and a neighbour passed the evening nursing mugs of wine out on deck.

And so we found out that this man's family used to farm our land, way back in the 1950's, and rented the house to a couple who now live just over the hill from us. I have also been told that the house itself was completely rebuilt in 1920, and moved further inland while they were at it. The site of the old house, and water mill, was right down by the sea in what is now our new hay field.

Because the house was moved there is no ruin to mark the place. But when we ploughed the field earlier this year we found a hoard of broken crockery and pieces of old, thick glass. Meanwhile, down on the shoreline the February gales exposed hundreds of slabs of old roofing slate, the real old heavy stuff with holes for wooden pegs. Some still contained fragments of wood.

I have kept the crockery. It holds an inexplicable fascination for me. Most of it is of the blue and white patterned variety and within each tiny fragment can be seen a leaf design, or a scrap of poetry, or the head of a Chinaman, or a shepherdess in full skirts and bonnet. There are a few pieces of what must have been a large, heavy casserole dish. It is made of thick terracotta, glazed only on the inside in a pale crème. As I hold its chunky remains, I can almost smell the steam of a meat and veggie hotpot.

All in all, through working the land and passing the time of day with the good folk of Sanday, we feel we're getting to know our farm rather well. I'm sure that if I spent a bit of time trawling through archived documentation I could find out the names of every person who ever lived here, but I'm rather enjoying this more organic route to the knowledge and have the pleasure of living in a community where that is still possible.

Fall ~ *August*

This morning I opened the shower door to the sound of geese flying overhead. With no thought for the trail of water I was creating, I rushed through the house to our new sun-room doors and stepped out into the garden to scan the sky. And there they were: maybe a hundred geese, forming a classic vee as they swept over the north end of our island.

Shom mishtake shurely? It's only August and we haven't, so far, even had a season that could be accurately described as summer. Migratory geese herald autumn as clearly as the cuckoo heralds spring. It's just not fair of them to arrive yet.

As if in collusion with the geese, a mail order catalogue company saw fit to send out their Christmas issue this week. This is really not on. I have a lot to do before winter sets in, not least of which is the need to soak up some sun. I am now pinning my hopes on an Indian summer.

But I mustn't grumble. The boys have had an excellent summer holiday with the usual plethora of activities laid on by our inexhaustible school staff. Fiddle Club summer school set the pace with a week of hard graft rewarded by the joy of good music, good food and good company. Through the rain of July our stoic boys cycled to school to have a go at felt-making, cake-decorating, pottery, karate, octopush, trampolining, rock pooling and ice-skating. Through the slightly drier rains of August they have indulged in climbing, canoeing, kayaking, camping, raft building, fencing and archery. Whatever the activity, they always seem to come home dripping wet and with a back-pack of wet clothes to boot. Our pulley is constantly laden. The six page summer activity timetable pinned to our kitchen wall reliably informs us that we will get to see the boys next week, for some quality family time before school re-starts.

A small plus to this year's poor weather is that I find sun cream on sale wherever I go. Factor 50 sun block, which is what my photo-sensitive horse needs slathered all over her nose on a daily basis, can be easily found in every chemist shop across Scotland on offer on a two-for-one basis.

The maxim "make hay while the sun shines" took on a grim irony in this past fortnight, as we watched our Orkney weather play cruelly with our haymaking efforts. Enough sun to persuade us to mow was followed by deluges of rain worthy of the tropics and interspersed with a cutting wind sent from Siberia. The latter did, at least, dry the sodden clumps of grass enough to call it hay. Another glimpse of sun prompted our friends with a baler to come and bale the stuff, which then enjoyed 24 hours of refreshingly light drizzle, just in case it was in danger of achieving that crisp dryness so desirable in one's winter hay store.

Suffice it to say that I'm looking into the pros and cons of making haylage next year. Haylage is made by cutting your hay field as normal but baling it when it is only 70% dry. The resultant matter, once plastic wrapped, ferments slightly and thus preserves itself, is not dusty and retains a whole lot more of the nutrients of fresh grass. Those are the pros which, in this dodgy Orkney climate would suggest that haylage is the crop for us. The cons include the need for a whole new set of machinery and a small but catastrophic risk of botulism: the atmosphere in the wrapped bales is perfect for growth of the bacterium Clostridium botulinum. That's a decision to ponder through the long winter months.

Speaking of which, I was shocked to discover that we are no longer in the season of the midnight sun. Last night, due to a myriad of mundane tasks, I didn't set out on my bedtime round of shutting in the hens, walking the dogs, checking the sheep, scratching the pigs and stroking the horses until 10pm. A veil of velvet darkness draped itself around me. Perhaps the geese are right. These nights are fair drawing in.

Chooks - *August*

There is so much to learn about this farming life and we haven't been at it for long. Only last October did we start the ball rolling with the purchase of 56 ewes and a ram. Having always assumed I would be a grower of plants - vegetables, herbs, fruit, even cereals - we found ourselves, instead, in the business of growing meat. Our first lambing was tough (for us) but successful and we are now in possession of around one hundred lambs destined for the journey across Orkney's wild waters to Kirkwall's Auction Mart sometime this autumn.

Ah well, we reasoned, we might as well be hung for a sheep as a lamb. If we are going to raise our own meat, to both eat and sell, we might as well introduce some variety into our diet. We bought piglets, to be raised for the freezer, where they will be very shortly. Recently we started incubating our own hens' eggs and growing on the hatched chicks, also with an eye to our Sunday menus. It seemed silly to be buying in chicken when we had the resources to grow our own.

Today is B-day for the first batch of chickens. If you are feint-hearted or morally strident about killing animals for food, you may want to stop reading at this point. We are ready. Our bedtime reading for the previous few nights has revolved around chapter five (Butchering Day) of Storey's Guide to Raising Chickens, and the poultry section of Hugh Fearnley-Whittingstall's River Cottage Cookbook. Perusing the given weaponry choices for killing a chicken - knife, gun, axe or hand - we both chose the simplest and most honest sounding one - hand.

We have set out our stall well away from our flock of live chickens. We have the chosen four in a small cage on the floor, covered by a blanket to give them the impression of darkness. Nic lifts the first, reluctant, chook out of the cage and between the two of us (neither wants the blame) we quickly wring its neck. This is the part we were most worried about, but it's a surprisingly easy manoeuvre. Too easy, really. More of a struggle might have resulted in more of a feeling of victory, and less one of sadness and guilt.

As we break the neck of each chicken we pop it into a cardboard box to allow it its final muscle spasms without having to watch it run around the byre. Way back when I was freshly out of university, I took a summer job which involved living at the top of Glen Doll, in Scotland's Angus Glens. The farm where my caravan was sited was run by a real salt-of-the-earth couple, who looked after me very well. I used to watch in fascination as Mrs. Brown, (in the autumn of her years, I'm sure she wouldn't mind my saying) came out of her kitchen in spotless flowery pinny, grabbed a passing chicken and had its head on a tree stump and her axe on its head in one deft move. The headless chook would then run free for a full circuit of the yard before collapsing.

With the chooks strung up by their legs we bleed them (slit their throats) and then start to pluck. This, we discover, is also fairly easy, although how the fastest known plucking time of 4.5 seconds was achieved I just cannot imagine. After a good ten minutes we are beginning to flag. We both admit that we hate this task. This isn't the moment to chicken out - having killed the birds we must at least eat them - but it is one of those rare moments of extreme clarity. This is not, we decide, something we want to make a habit of.

I'm pleased that we have killed and eaten (I've just finished some very tasty fried chicken) our own produce. As an animal-raising, meat-eating farmer it makes sense to be able to complete the whole process. But we have now put butchering into the category of "tasks to leave to the experts" along with such things as vehicle mechanics, dentistry and piloting aircraft. As I said, there's an endless amount to learn about farming and not least of it is learning how and what one wants to farm.

Haylage - *September*

Time and tide, hay and sunshine, wait for no man. I was going to use this week to do some crop research, but then the rain stopped and the sun came out and hay making was on. Or in our case haylage. With three hundred square bales already in the byre from our August efforts, this was our chance to have a go at a batch of haylage with our remaining two acres of uncut grass.

On Tuesday we went to town on the ferry with a bunch of cast ewes (old sheep who are no longer useful members of the breeding flock) and Nic and his Dad, grinning like a couple of dodgy dealers, took them to the Mart to sell. I left them to it. I had to see a woman about a horse. We reconvened on our homebound ferry, the lads brandishing their pathetic winnings with wry, waning, grins. Our sheep had barely covered the cost of their own transport, poor things.

On Wednesday we considered the glowering skies and decided to go for it. While Nic hitched mower to tractor and started cutting, I hiked off up the back track and along Lopness beach for my fiddle lesson. By the time I returned the shorn grass lay in neat rows and Nic was rooting in the kitchen for something edible. Twenty minutes later the heavens opened, thunder and lightening to boot.

On Thursday we hitched up the trailer once again and bedded it down with straw. Feeling like traitors to their trust, we cajoled our lovely, friendly, Large White pigs into it and tucked them up in the front pen. Having spent a happy six months romping around in our three acre beach field, it was definitely time they went to Never Never Land. At Kirkwall we paused on the weigh bridge both before and after unloading the pigs and thus worked out their combined weight of 260kg. I think we might need a bigger freezer for that lot.

Friday dawned with the possibility of a fine spell and we began to risk thoughts of gathering in our haylage. While Nic turned the hay over with the hay bob, I groomed and tacked up our two gorgeous Clydesdale horses. What with music, horses and children to fill my days, I'm not sure I could claim to do an awful lot of hands-on farming. With the hay turned and the sun shining warily through retreating storm clouds, we set off toward the glistening ocean on our magnificent steeds. It's a tough life.

By Saturday we were squinting and reaching for our long forgotten sunglasses. Summer had graced us with a flying visit. Out in the hay field the drying grass was at the perfect stage for haylage - nearly, but not quite dried through and smelling wonderfully aromatic. Time to row it up with the hay bob and wheel out the old round baler, which Nic had proudly rumbled home with after a shopping trip in Kirkwall a few weeks ago.

There is probably nothing quite so frustrating in a farmer's life than a perfect hay-making day coupled with a jammed baler. But, as an old hand up the road told us, this is par for the course. Having just started harvesting his barley he reckons to achieve twenty minutes of combining for every hour of machine maintenance (all the tweaking, bodging and kicking that these ancient, rust ridden machines need). And so it was with our round baler, until we learnt her whimsical ways. We made one good bale then couldn't get the string system to work. We called in an expert (yet another helpful neighbour) who sorted that.

Buoyed up by his visit we trundled on, watching with naive fascination as our baler munched up the rows of grass and rolled the mass of vegetation around in her belly. Then, like an over-stuffed gourmand, she seized up. The rollers stopped rolling, the shear pin sheared and the hood remained resolutely jammed shut. We ruminated the problem for a while and then fetched the Landrover and a tow rope. Sometimes (most times) brute force is the only solution. Having pulled open the hood to deliver her five foot round baby, we spent the next glorious three hours yanking thick wodges of grass/hay from between all the jammed rollers. The air was as blue as the sky.

As we got going again Ian arrived to help wrap the bales, assuming we'd be ready for him by now. He saw in an instant our mistake and ran over to shout to Nic in the tractor cab. Keep the revs up, was all he said. And there we had it, the last but vital little key to success. By nightfall we had fifteen wrapped bales of haylage stacked along the byre wall. The first raindrops fell as we chinked beer bottles.

Books by Julia Welstead

In *Fine that ~ an Orkney island life* Julia Welstead describes the joys and the pitfalls of her move from a city life in Edinburgh to the remote and idyllic island of Sanday, in the northern archipelago of Orkney. These gritty and honest accounts of her journey are interspersed with an evocative selection of full colour photographs and sketches of the beautiful Orkney Islands by Moonart. 160 pages, 11 x 9 inch (28 x 23cm), full colour.

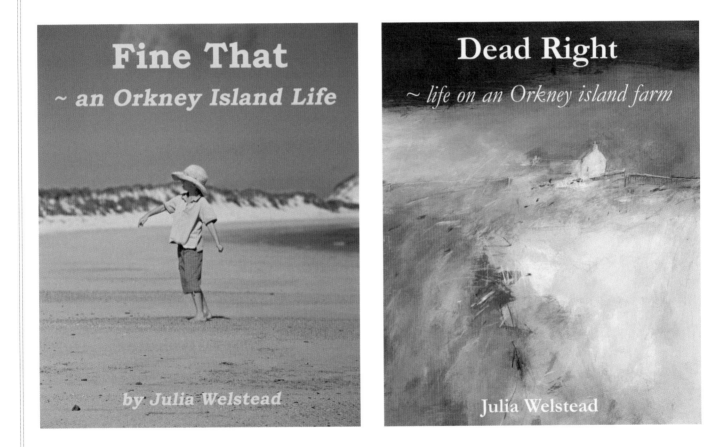

In *Dead Right ~ life on an Orkney island farm* Julia Welstead and her family have settled in to life on Sanday and taken on the additional challenge of running a fifty acre, coastal farm, armed with nothing more than enthusiasm, determination and a good measure of humour. Fellow islander Dominique Cameron has astutely captured the essence of the island with her vivid and stunning paintings and photographs. 160 pages, 10 x 8 inch (26 x 21cm), full colour.

Published by Treb Ltd.

Treb Publishing

Order Form

Telephone Orders: Call 01857 600755 (All major credit cards accepted)

email orders: orders@trebpublishing.com

Internet orders: www.trebpublishing.com

Cheques with this form to: Treb Ltd, Crudy, Sanday, Orkney, KW17 2BP

Please send me the following books :

___ Book(s) ~ Dead Right   @ £ 14.99 each   £ _____
      life on an Orkney island farm

___ Book(s) ~ Fine That   @ £ 14.99 each   £ _____
      an Orkney island life

___ Pair(s) ~ Fine That & Dead Right combined   @ £ 26.98 pair   £ _____

_1_ Postage & packing for the 1st copy   @ £ 2.00   £ ___ 2 - 00

___ Extra postage per additional copy   @ £ 1.00   £ _____
      (to same address)

Total due now for this order   £ _____

(e.g. the total for 1 copy of Dead Right would be £16.99 delivered, the total for 1 copy of each book would be £29.98 delivered)

Name   _____

Address   _____

      _____

Town   _____

County   _____

Post Code   _____

Phone   _____

Email   _____

Date   _____

You should receive your delivery within 7 days of receipt of order.

Thank you for your order and we hope you enjoy the books.